MW01680100

WORDPERFECT® 6.1 FOR WINDOWS®

Sarah E. Hutchinson
Glen J. Coulthard
Catherine Schuler

THE IRWIN ADVANTAGE SERIES
FOR COMPUTER EDUCATION

♦

IRWIN

Chicago • Bogotá • Boston • Buenos Aires • Caracas
London • Madrid • Mexico City • Sydney • Toronto

Printed in the United States of America.

ISBN 0-256-19433-5

2 3 4 5 6 7 8 9 0 ML 2 1 0 9 8 7 6 5

Table of Contents

Session 1: Fundamentals

SESSION 2: FORMATTING COMMANDS

SESSION 3: EDITING AND PROOFING TOOLS

Session 4: Printing and File Management Commands

SESSION 5: ADVANCED FEATURES

USING THIS GUIDE

This tutorial is one in a series of learning guides that lead you through the most popular microcomputer software programs available. Concepts, skills, and procedures are grouped into session topics and are presented in a logical and structured manner. Commands and procedures are introduced using hands-on examples, and you are encouraged to perform the steps along with the guide. Although you may turn directly to a later session, be aware that some sessions require, or at least assume, that you have completed the previous sessions. For maximum benefit, you should work through the short-answer and hands-on exercises appearing at the end of each session.

The exercises and examples in this guide use several standard conventions to indicate menu instructions, keystroke combinations, and command instructions.

MENU INSTRUCTIONS

When you need to execute a command from a menu, the tutorial's instruction line uses a comma to separate menu options. For example, the command for saving a file is shown as:

> CHOOSE: File, Save

This instruction tells you to press the F key to choose the File option and then the S key to choose the Save option. Keys separated by commas are not pressed at the same time.

KEYSTROKES AND KEYSTROKE COMBINATIONS

When you must press two keys together, the tutorial's instruction line shows the keys joined with a plus sign (+). For example, to move the cursor a screen to the right, hold down **Shift** and then press **Tab**. The instruction for using this command is shown as:

> PRESS: **Shift**+**Tab**

Command Instructions

This guide indicates with a special typeface data that you are required to type in yourself. For example:

TYPE: `George Washington`

When you are required to enter unique information, such as the current date or your name, the instructions appear in italics. The following instruction directs you to type your name in place of the actual words: "your name."

TYPE: *`your name`*

Instructions that use general directions rather than a specific option or command name appear italicized in the regular typeface.

PRESS: *the cursor-movement keys to highlight the text*

Advantage Diskette

The Advantage Diskette, provided with this guide or by your instructor, contains the files that you use in each session and in the hands-on exercises. This diskette is extremely important for ensuring the success of the guide.

If you are using this guide in a self-study program, we suggest that you make a copy of the Advantage Diskette using the DOS DISKCOPY command. When the guide asks you to insert the Advantage Diskette, you insert and work with the copied diskette instead. By following this procedure, you will be able to work through the guide again at a later date using a fresh copy of the Advantage Diskette. For more information on using the DISKCOPY command, please refer to your DOS manual.

SESSION 1

WORDPERFECT 6.1 FOR WINDOWS: FUNDAMENTALS

Word processing is the most popular application for microcomputers. Whether you write term papers, business plans, or letters to your Aunt Sally, a word processing software package lets you easily create, edit, format, and permanently store documents. In the educational and business communities, you are often expected to use a computer and word processor to create your work—handwritten correspondence just isn't acceptable in these formal environments. In this session, you explore the features and benefits of word processing using Windows and Novell's WordPerfect 6.1.

PREVIEW

When you have completed this session, you will be able to:

Describe several features of word processing software and the benefits of WordPerfect for Windows

•

Load Windows and start WordPerfect for Windows

•

Describe the WordPerfect screen and the menu system

•

Enter, edit, and erase text in a document and access the Help facility

•

Save, close, and retrieve documents

•

Exit WordPerfect and Windows

Session Outline

WHY IS THIS SESSION IMPORTANT?

This guide leads you step-by-step through using one of the most popular word processing programs available for Microsoft Windows—WordPerfect 6.1 for Windows. You will initially concentrate on word processing fundamentals and then explore the basic procedures, commands, and utilities required to work effectively with WordPerfect for Windows. This session introduces word processing terminology and procedures, and lets you practice creating, saving, and retrieving documents.

Word processing is the most commonly used application for microcomputers and is often cited as the primary reason for purchasing a computer. Briefly stated, **word processing** is the method by which documents (for example, letters, reports, and other correspondence) are created, edited, formatted, and printed. Although the process of creating a document using a word processing software program is similar to using a typewriter, the methods for editing documents differ greatly. With a typewriter, any changes you make—correcting typos, deleting words or sentences, adding or enhancing text—require you to retype the entire page or pages. Word processing programs, on the other hand, enable you to make changes without retyping any pages, as well as retrieve, edit, and reprint documents quickly and easily.

Some of the more popular word processing software programs include Novell's WordPerfect, Microsoft Word, and Ami Pro. These programs provide not only basic word processing tools but also publishing capabilities previously limited to commercial typesetters and printers. Let's begin exploring the features of word processing.

Before proceeding, make sure the following are true:

1. You have access to WordPerfect 6.1 for Windows.
2. Your Advantage Diskette is inserted into either drive A: or drive B:. You will save your work onto the diskette and retrieve files that have been created for you. (*Note*: The Advantage Diskette can be duplicated by copying all the files from your instructor's Master Advantage Diskette.)

WORD PROCESSING WITH MICROCOMPUTERS

This section describes the basics of working with word processing software. Beginning with a general discussion of how to create and edit a document, the section proceeds to more advanced issues, such as merging mailing lists with form letters.

ENTERING TEXT

A document is created in a word processing program by typing information into the system that is displayed on the screen. However, the document is not permanently stored until you save the document to the hard disk or to a floppy diskette. Saving your work to a disk is similar to photocopying a document and placing it into a filing cabinet. Of course, when stored electronically on a disk, a document can be retrieved much faster than it can when it is stored in a filing cabinet.

When you begin typing, information is entered into a document at the **cursor** position. The cursor, sometimes called an *insertion point* in Windows, is displayed on the screen as a flashing underline or vertical bar. You use the cursor-movement keys and the mouse to position the cursor in the document before you insert, delete, or select text.

Text is entered into a document in one of two modes: Insert mode or Typeover mode. **Insert mode** inserts text at the cursor position and pushes existing text to the right. **Typeover mode** inserts text *in place of* existing text. In most word processing programs, you press Insert to toggle (switch) between modes.

Novices and experts alike make typing errors when creating a document. As you type, you can correct errors by using BackSpace and Delete and then retyping the desired text. BackSpace removes the character or space to the left of the cursor each time BackSpace is pressed, and Delete removes text to the right of the cursor. Although these keys are useful for deleting text one character at a time, more efficient methods for deleting blocks of text are introduced later in the guide.

Another convenient feature of computer-based word processing is called **word wrap**. Word wrap is the process of automatically moving the cursor to the next line when the end of the current line is reached. In other words, you may continuously type without worrying about pressing Enter to advance to the next line. **Enter** is used to end paragraphs and insert blank lines in a document.

Editing Text

Word processing programs have numerous editing features to assist you in making corrections and modifications to existing documents. Two of the most important features involve methods for inserting, deleting, and rearranging text. First, Insert mode, as described above, enables you to insert text anywhere in a document. This process works well for inserting a sentence or phrase in the middle of an existing paragraph. Second, the copy and move functions allow you to change the order of paragraphs or sections in a document and limit the need to retype similar information. (You will practice copy and move functions in Session 3.)

Some word processing programs even possess sophisticated search and replace capabilities for changing information throughout an entire document. These editing features are often underutilized; being aware of them is the first step to becoming an efficient user of word processing software.

Formatting

Formatting refers to establishing or changing the appearance of text in a document. There are four different levels of formatting that may be applied to text.

1. *Character formatting selects typefaces and type sizes for text.*
   The most common way to emphasize text is to apply boldface, italic, or underline character-formatting styles.

2. *Paragraph formatting specifies text alignment, line spacing, indentations, and tab settings.*
   A paragraph can be a single line of text, an entire page of text, or perhaps several pages in a document. Each paragraph may be formatted independently from the rest of the document.

3. *Section formatting inserts page numbers, headers, and footers.*
   When a document is divided into chapters, section formatting commands apply the different headers, footers, and page numbers.

4. *Document formatting specifies the overall page layout.*
   Formatting topics at this level include choosing the paper size, page orientation (vertical or horizontal), and margins.

These formatting options are discussed in detail throughout this guide.

PROOFING TOOLS

Most word processing programs offer spell-checking capabilities. When you request a spelling check of a document, the word processing program loads a standard spelling dictionary into the computer's memory. Each word in the document is then compared to the words stored in the dictionary. If no match is found for a word, the **spelling checker** typically marks the word and suggests a list of correctly spelled words. In the following example, the Spell Checker has found a suggested spelling for the misspelled word "superfulous."

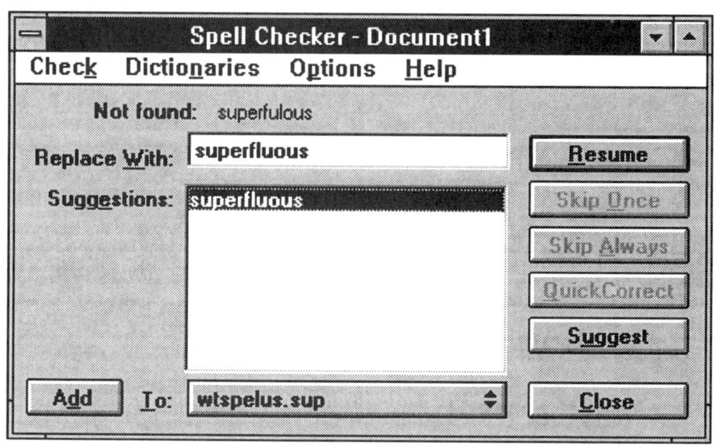

At this point, you can type in a new word, accept a word from the presented list, or keep your original word. Many programs also offer the ability to create custom dictionaries for storing proper names, special terminology, and abbreviations.

Another writing tool commonly found in word processing programs is the electronic thesaurus. A **thesaurus** provides a list of synonyms (words of similar meaning) for a given word or phrase. As with the spelling checker, you can type in a new word, accept a word from the presented list of synonyms, or keep your original word. In the following example, the thesaurus has found a list of words that have a similar meaning to "superfluous":

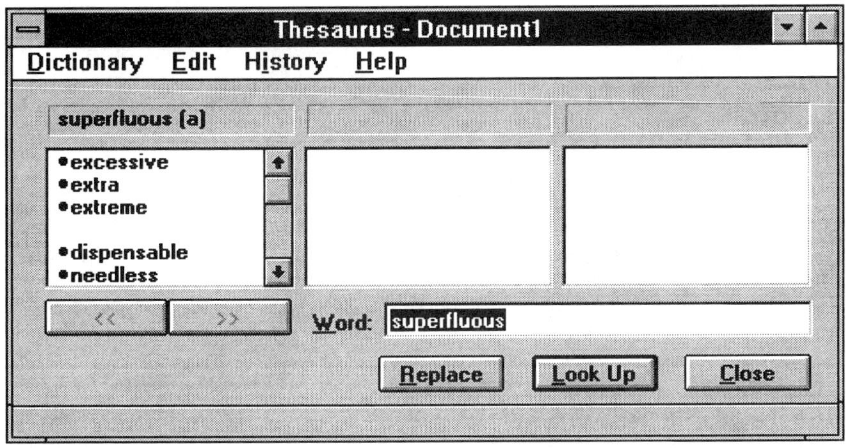

WordPerfect also incorporates the use of a full-featured **grammar checker**, called Grammatik, to analyze punctuation, sentence structure, and word usage.

PRINTING

After creating, editing, formatting, and proofing a document, you'll usually want to send it to the printer. Before performing this step, you should make sure your computer is connected to a printer. Your options for printing a document often include printing multiple copies and limiting the print selection to specific pages. Most word processing programs also allow you to preview a document onscreen before printing. Besides saving trees, this feature allows you to see the effects of formatting changes without having to print the document.

MERGING

One of the most powerful features of word processing software is the ability to merge names and addresses into standard documents for printing. This process, called **mail merge**, allows you to create a single document and then print personalized copies of that document for numerous recipients. However, mail merge activities are not limited to producing form letters. Merging can be used to print a batch of invoices, contract letters, legal documents, or proposals. The merging process is covered in Session 5 of this guide.

THE WINDOWS ADVANTAGE

WordPerfect for Windows is one of the best-selling word processing software programs for the Windows environment. With over 10 million copies of Windows sold in the last few years, Windows is the environment of choice for many personal computer users. This section explains some of the benefits and shortcomings of working in the Windows environment.

Microsoft Windows is a software program that works with DOS to provide a **graphical user interface (GUI)** for programs. This GUI interface is designed to make using computers easier and more intuitive. With Windows, you use a pointing device called a **mouse** to select from **icons** (pictures that represent programs or functions) rather than typing lengthy commands.

Some other advantages of working in the Windows environment are these these factors:

1. *Windows programs are easy to learn and easy to use.*
   Windows provides a standardized interface for all programs, whether they are word processing, spreadsheet, or database applications. As a result, you can use the knowledge acquired from one Windows product in working with other Windows products.

2. *The ability to run more than one application at a time.*
   Windows is a **multitasking** environment whereby more than one application or program may be run at the same time. This feature is especially important for electronic mail, modem, or fax programs that must be loaded in the computer's memory to inform you of incoming transactions while you are working on something else—creating a document, for example. Multitasking allows you to simultaneously look through a document or spreadsheet in one application while working in another.

3. *The ability to exchange information among applications.*
   Windows provides a program called the **Clipboard** to copy and move information within an application or among applications. Because

more than one application can be running at the same time, you can, for instance, copy a budget from an Excel spreadsheet to the Clipboard and then paste that budget from the Clipboard into a report written in WordPerfect for Windows.

4. *The ability to display on the screen what you will get from the printer.* This feature is called **WYSIWYG** ("What You See Is What You Get") and allows different fonts, borders, and graphics to be displayed on the screen at all times. Most DOS programs provide a print preview feature but do not display the true WYSIWYG capabilities of Windows programs.

WHAT'S NEW IN WORDPERFECT 6.1 FOR WINDOWS

At the time of this writing, the latest release of WordPerfect for Windows is Version 6.1. WordPerfect 6.1 is now incorporated as part of the Novell PerfectOffice suite of products and can be used as part of this integrated software package or as a stand-alone word processor. To ensure competitiveness in the marketplace WordPerfect introduced several significant features in Version 6.1. This section highlights some of these enhancements.

- WordPerfect 6.1 is part of the Novell PerfectOffice integrated software package in which all programs have consistent menus, toobars and key dialog boxes.

- WordPerfect 6.1 supports OLE 2.0 (object linking and embedding) allowing you to drag and drop information to and from other PerfectOffice or OLE 2.0 applications.

- New Document Experts let you create professional business documents simply by filling in the blanks. Experts are available to create tables and the Make It Fit Expert shrinks or expands a document to fit a specified number of pages.

- An enhanced QuickCorrect utility corrects spelling, capitalization and spacing errors while typing.

- PerfectSense technology has been applied to the Find and Replace utility allowing you to search for and replace not only words, but word forms, embedded codes, and character formatting.

- Coaches are available to help with learning specific tasks and an Upgrade Expert is ready to help compare feature names with those used in competitive products or in previous WordPerfect versions.

If you are new to word processing, you may not understand all of the terms used in the above discussion. Don't despair - you'll definitely understand the importance of these features by the end of this guide. Now, let's begin our journey through WordPerfect 6.1 for Windows.

WORKING WITH WORDPERFECT FOR WINDOWS

WordPerfect 6.1 is a complex yet easy-to-learn program. As you proceed through this guide, you will find that there are often three methods for performing the same command or procedure in WordPerfect:

- Menu — Select a command or procedure from the Menu bar
- Mouse — Point to and click a toolbar button
- Keyboard — Press a keyboard shortcut (usually Ctrl+a letter)

HOW THE MOUSE IS USED IN WORDPERFECT

The mouse is an essential tool for working in the Windows environment. Although it is possible to use WordPerfect with only a keyboard, much of the program's basic design revolves around the use of a mouse. *Note*: In WordPerfect, some commands can be accessed only with a mouse. Although your mouse may have two or three buttons, WordPerfect primarily uses the left mouse button for selecting items and commands.

The mouse actions used in WordPerfect are:

- Point — Slide the mouse on your desk to position the tip of the mouse pointer over the desired object on the screen.

- Click — Press down and release the left mouse button quickly. Clicking is used to position the cursor in the document and to choose options from a dialog box.
- Double-Click — Press down and release the left mouse button twice in rapid succession. Double-clicking is often used to select and execute an action.
- Drag — Press down and hold the left mouse button as you move the mouse pointer across the screen. When the mouse pointer reaches the desired location, release the mouse button. Dragging is used to select a block of text or to move items or windows.

You may notice that the mouse pointer changes shape as you move the mouse over different parts of the screen. Each mouse pointer shape has its own purpose and may provide you with important information. There are three primary mouse pointer shapes:

	Left arrow	Used to choose menu items or make selections from the Tool and Power bars, and dialog boxes.
	Hourglass	Used to inform you that WordPerfect is occupied with another task and to request that you wait.
	I-beam	Used to modify and edit text, and to position the cursor.

As you proceed through this guide, other mouse shapes will be explained as they appear.

How the Keyboard Is Used in WordPerfect

Aside from being the primary input device for creating a document, the keyboard offers shortcut methods for performing commands and procedures. Several menu commands have shortcut key combinations listed to the right of the command in the pull-down menu. For example, instead of choosing the Speller option from the Menu bar, you could simply press Ctrl+F1. Many of these shortcut key combinations are available throughout Windows applications.

WordPerfect for Windows assigns commonly used commands to function keys. Most of these commands will be explained later in the guide.

STARTING WORDPERFECT FOR WINDOWS

Because Microsoft Windows requires a hard disk, this session assumes that you are working on a computer with DOS, Windows, and WordPerfect 6.1 for Windows loaded on the hard disk drive. In most cases, the hard disk of a personal computer is drive C:. The Windows program is stored in a directory on the hard disk called \WINDOWS, much like in a reserved drawer in a filing cabinet.

Before using WordPerfect, you must turn on the computer and load Microsoft Windows. Perform the following steps on your computer to begin working with WordPerfect for Windows:

1. Turn on the power switches to the computer and monitor. The C:\> prompt or a menu appears announcing that your computer has successfully loaded the Disk Operating System (DOS). (*Note*: If your computer automatically loads Microsoft Windows when it is started, you can move on to step 3.)

2. To start Microsoft Windows from the C:\> prompt:
   TYPE: `WIN`
   PRESS: Enter
   After a few seconds, the Windows logo appears on the screen followed by the Program Manager window (Figure 1.1). (*Note*: The icons in your Program Manager window may not be exactly the same as in Figure 1.1; the icons represent the programs stored on your hard disk.)

3. To start WordPerfect for Windows from the Program Manager, first open the WordPerfect for Windows group in the **Program Manager** window:
   DOUBLE-CLICK: *WPWin 6.1 group icon*

If a mouse is not available, press Ctrl+Tab until the WPWin 6.1 group icon is highlighted and then press Enter.

4. Load WordPerfect from the WordPerfect for Windows group window (Figure 1.2):
   DOUBLE-CLICK: *WPWin 6.1 program icon*
   If a mouse is not available, press the cursor-movement keys until the WPWin 6.1 program icon is highlighted and then press Enter.

Figure 1.1

The Microsoft Windows Program Manager

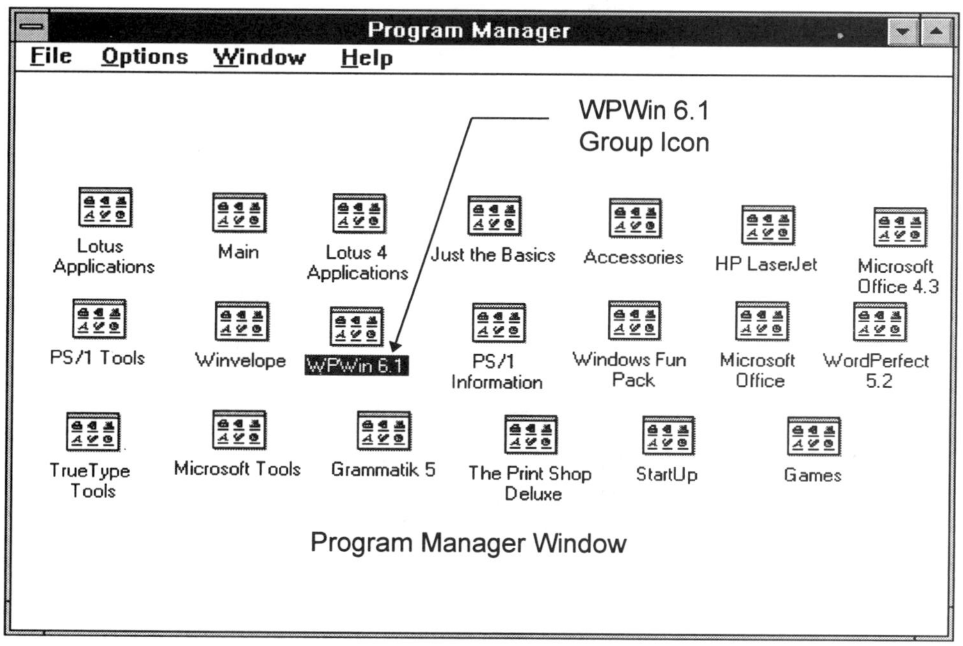

Figure 1.2

The WPWin 6.1 Group Window

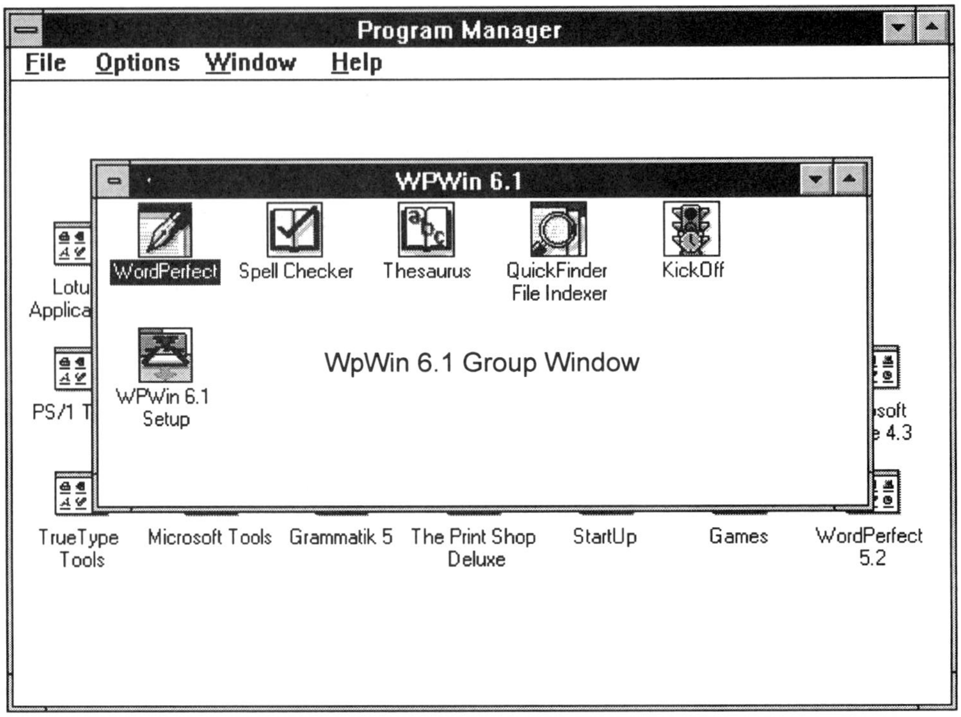

Quick Reference
Starting Windows and Loading WordPerfect

1. To start Windows from the C:\> prompt:
   TYPE: `WIN` and then press **Enter**.
2. To start WordPerfect for Windows from the Program Manager:
   a. Using a mouse, double-click on the WPWin 6.1 group icon and then double-click on the WPWin 6.1 program icon.
   b. Using the keyboard, press **Ctrl**+**Tab** until the WPWin 6.1 group icon is highlighted and then press **Enter**. Use the arrow keys to highlight the WPWin 6.1 program icon and press **Enter** to start the program.

THE GUIDED TOUR

Software programs designed for Microsoft Windows, such as WordPerfect for Windows, Excel, and PageMaker, have many similarities in screen design and layout. Each program operates in its own Application window when running under Windows. Within an application, each letter, spreadsheet, or brochure that you create appears in its own Document window. This section explores the various parts of WordPerfect for

Windows including the tools for manipulating Application and Document windows.

APPLICATION WINDOW

The WordPerfect for Windows screen consists of the **application window** and the **document window**. The application window (Figure 1.3) contains the Title bar, Menu bar, Toolbar, Power bar, Status bar, and document window. Document windows, which are described in more detail shortly, contain the workspace where you type in document information (such as a letter) that you will later save onto a disk. In the Application window, you can have multiple document windows open at the same time. In other words, WordPerfect enables you to work on more than one document at a time.

Figure 1.3

The Application window

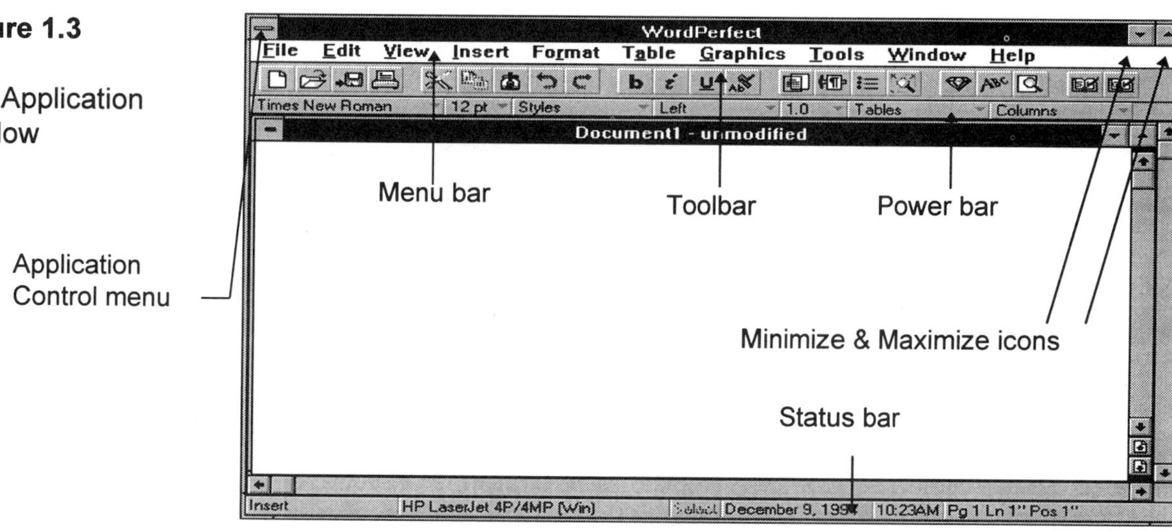

The primary components of the application window are:

Application Control menu (▬)	Used to size and position the application window using the keyboard. To quit WordPerfect, you can double-click the Application Control menu.

Minimize (▼) and Maximize (▲) or Restore (⬍) icons	Located in the top right-hand corner of the application window, these triangular-shaped icons are used to control the display of the application window using the mouse.
Title bar	The Title bar contains the name of the program or document file. Using a mouse, you can move a window by dragging its Title bar.
Menu bar	Contains the WordPerfect menu commands.
Toolbar	The Toolbar gives you quick access to commonly used word processing commands. (Discussed later in this session.)
Power bar	The Power bar is located below the Toolbar and provides you will quick access to editing commands.
Status bar	Located at the bottom of the application window, the Status bar displays status or mode information and tracks your current position in the document. (Discussed shortly.)

Document Window

The Document window provides the viewing and editing area for a document. When WordPerfect for Windows is first loaded, the Document window is empty; think of the Document window at this point as a blank piece of paper. Also, when WordPerfect for Windows is first loaded, the Document window is maximized to fill the entire document area of the Application window (Figure 1.4).

Figure 1.4

The Document window at maximum size

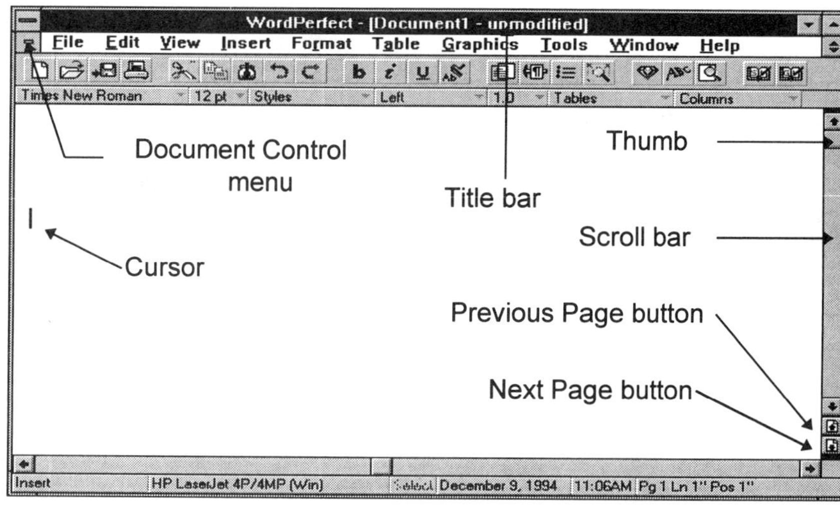

The parts of the document window are:

Document Control menu (▬)	Used to size and position the window using the keyboard. To close a document, you can double-click the Document Control menu.
Scroll bar	A scroll bar appears at the right border of the Document window. You can use the scroll bar to move through a document using the mouse, by clicking the arrow heads at either end of a scroll bar or by dragging the "Thumb" up and down the scroll bar.
Previous Page/Next Page buttons	Also, located on the bottom of the vertical scroll bar, the Previous Page button (▣) enables you to move the cursor to the previous page (in a multi-page document) and the Next Page button (▣) enables you to move the cursor to the next page.

You should recognize some familiar components in the document window that appear in all windows. For example, the Minimize and Maximize icons appear in the top right-hand corner of the document window. To restore a maximized document to a winodw, you click the Restore icon (⬍). To maximize the document window, you click the Maximize icon (▲). Before proceeding, makde sure that your document window is maximized, resembling Figure 1.4.

Menu Bar

WordPerfect commands are grouped together on the Menu bar, as shown below.

Commands in this guide are written in the following form: *Edit*, *Copy*, where *Edit* is the Menu bar option and *Copy* is the command to be selected from the pull-down menu. To execute a command using the mouse, click once on the Menu bar option and then click once on the pull-down menu command. Using the keyboard, you hold down Alt and tap the underlined letter of the desired option on the Menu bar. When the pull-down menu is displayed, press the underlined letter of the command you want to execute. Commands that are not available for selection appear dimmed. Commands that are followed by an ellipsis (...) require further information to be collected in a dialog box.

Toolbar

The Toolbar provides quick and easy access to the more popular features of WordPerfect. Accessible using a mouse, the buttons on the Toolbar provide you with single-step functionality. Table 1.1 summarizes the buttons from left to right as they appear on the Toolbar.

Table 1.1

Toolbar

Button	Description
	Create a new document in a new window.
	Retrieve/open an existing document into a new window.
	Save the current document.
	Print the current document.
	Cut a block and place it in the Clipboard.

 Copy a block into the Clipboard.

 Paste the contents of the Clipboard into a document at the insertion point.

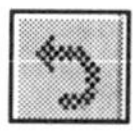 Undo button reverses the last change made to the document.

 Redo button reverses the last UNDO command made to the document.

 Turn on the bold font.

 Turn on the italics font.

 Turn on the underline font.

 QuickFormat. Apply the formatting of a paragraph or selected text to another paragraph or selected text.

 Creates a new document based on a template.

 Set paragraph formatting options.

 Insert bullets into a document.

 Make it Fit button. Shrink or expand a document to fit the page.

 Retrieve a graphics figure.

 Insert text art and special effects.

 Page/Zoom Full. View part of the document (Page view) or zoom out to see the full page (Zoom view)

 Speller. Check a document's spelling.

 Thesaurus. Use the Thesaurus feature.

	Grammatik. Check the document for proper grammar and spelling.
	Start the WordPerfect Coach to guide you in specific tasks.

POWER BAR

The Power bar displays information about the current font, style, justification, and line spacing. Tables and columns can be inserted from the Power bar. Like the buttons on the Toolbar, Power bar buttons are accessed using a mouse. Table 1.2 summarizes the buttons as they appear from left to right on the Power bar.

Table 1.2

Power bar

Button	Function
Times New Roman	Change the typeface of printed characters. The keyboard shortcut is F9.
12 pt	Change the size of printed characters.
Styles	Create a formatting style in a document or template.
Left	Align text in a document.
1.0	Change a document's line spacing.
Tables	Create a table.
Columns	Create columns.
100%	Zoom document in and out.

Status Bar

The Status bar displays information about the default printer, time, date, the current mode operation (Insert mode or Typeover mode) and whether a block of text has been selected.

WordPerfect also displays information on the Status bar that (among other things that we'll cover later) tells where the cursor is positioned in the document. In graphic above, note that the cursor is on Page 1 (Pg), Line 1" (Ln), and in position 3.14" (Pos). Unless you issue a command to change the margins in your document, WordPerfect will print your document with 1-inch margins on all sides of your document (top, bottom, left, and right); that is, by default, WordPerfect sets 1-inch margins on all sides of your document. (The term *default* refers to the assumptions made by a software program; in other words, default values are what you get unless you enter specific values of your own choosing.)

Dialog Box

WordPerfect uses dialog boxes (Figure 1.5) to collect information necessary to execute a command. When a command is followed by an ellipsis (...) on a pull-down menu, WordPerfect presents a dialog box upon selection of that command. (*Note*: When a command is followed by a sideways triangle, WordPerfect presents another pull-down menu upon selection of the command.) As mentioned earlier, dialog boxes are also used to display messages or ask for confirmation of commands.

Figure 1.5

A dialog box

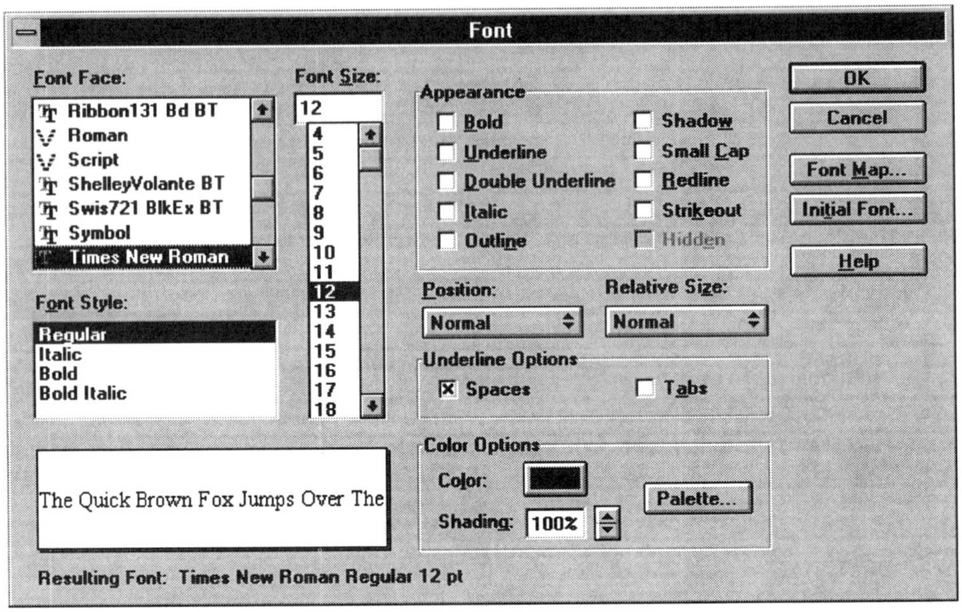

A dialog box uses several methods for collecting information including list boxes, text boxes, drop-down lists, check boxes, option buttons, and command buttons. You activate an item in the dialog box using a mouse, or by pressing Tab to move clockwise and Shift+Tab to move counter-clockwise around the dialog box.

Table 1.3 describes the various methods used for collecting information in dialog boxes.

Table 1.3

Parts of a Dialog Box

List Box	A scrollable list of choices. Use the scroll bars or cursor keys to browse the list.
Text Box	A box for collecting typed information. (*Note*: A text box that appears with an arrow to its right can also be used as a drop-down list box.)
Drop-Down List	A list of available choices in which only one item is displayed at a time. Using a mouse, click on the adjacent arrow to display the full list.

Check Box	An option that can be toggled (switched) on or off. Select the box and press the Space Bar to toggle the "X" mark on and off, or click on the box using a mouse.
Option Button	One option that can be selected from a group of related options.
Command Button	A button that executes an action when selected.

CREATING A DOCUMENT

Creating a document in WordPerfect for Windows is easy. You type information onto the screen, save the document to the disk, and then send it to the printer. Before entering text into the document, make sure that you have a blinking cursor, which looks like a vertical bar, near the top of the document window. The cursor is positioned where the first character you type will print on a piece of paper; that is, 1 inch from the left margin and 1 inch from the top of the page.

In this section, you'll create the paragraph in Figure 1.6.

Figure 1.6

Practice paragraph

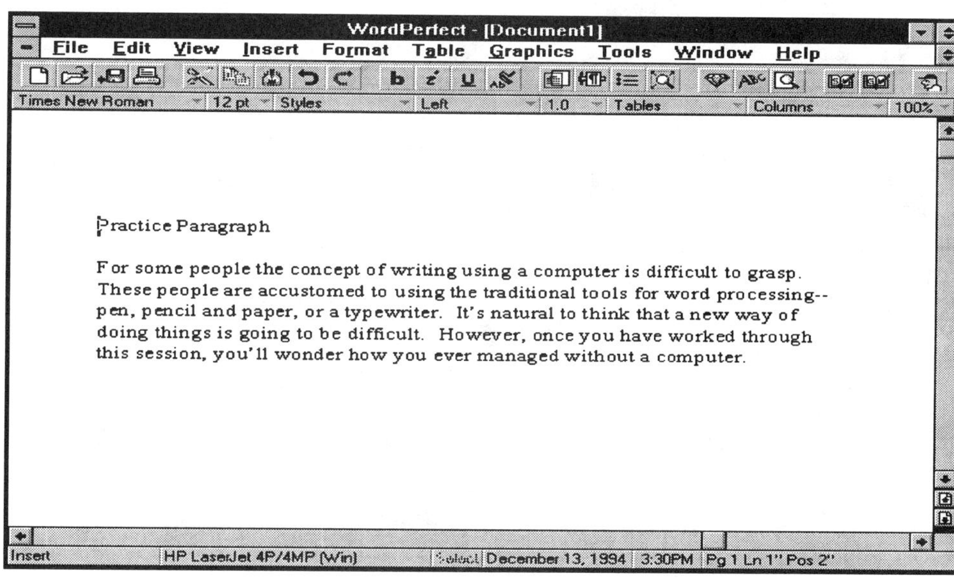

ENTERING TEXT

To illustrate the fundamentals of inserting text, this section leads you through a simple exercise for editing the words *Practice Paragraph.* Perform the following steps:

1. TYPE: `Paragraph`
   The cursor appears one character to the right of the word "Paragraph."

2. To move the cursor back to the beginning of the line:
   PRESS: **Home**
   The cursor appears to the left of the "P" in "Paragraph."

3. TYPE: `Practice`
   PRESS: Space Bar
   When you first load WordPerfect for Windows, text is entered using Insert mode; you can tell that WordPerfect is in Insert mode because "Insert" is displaying on the left side of the Status bar. Therefore, you can insert text or spaces at the current cursor position by simply typing the characters or pressing the Space Bar. As you type, the existing information is pushed to the right.

4. To illustrate the difference between Insert mode and Typeover mode:
   PRESS: **←** *a few times to position the cursor to the left of the "P" in the word "Practice."*

5. PRESS: **Insert**
   The text "Typeover," which stands for Typeover mode, appears on the Status bar.

6. TYPE: `My`
   The word "My" should have overwritten the first two characters of "Practice."

7. Let's complete the phrase:
   PRESS: **Insert** *to toggle Insert mode on*
   PRESS: Space Bar *to insert a space*
   TYPE: `Pr`
   The phrase now reads "My Practice Paragraph."

8. **Enter** inserts blank lines into a document and signifies the end of a paragraph. To illustrate, position the cursor to the left of the letter "P" in the word "Paragraph."

9. PRESS: [Enter] *four times*
   The word "Paragraph" moves down with the cursor and blank lines are inserted into the document. In the next section, you learn how to delete blank lines from a document.

Quick Reference
Entering Text

- Insert text into a document by typing.
- Insert spaces between words by pressing the Space Bar.
- Insert blank lines in a document by pressing [Enter].
- Press [Insert] to toggle between the Insert and Typeover modes for entering text.

Deleting Text

[BackSpace] and [Delete] are often used for removing information from a document one character at a time. To practice each keystroke, perform the following steps.

1. To quickly move to the top of the document:
   PRESS: [Ctrl]+[Home]
   The cursor jumps to the first column of the first line in the document.

2. To move to the end of line:
   PRESS: [End]

3. In order to get the word "Paragraph" back to its original location, you must delete the blank lines.
   PRESS: [Delete] *four times*

4. To illustrate the use of [BackSpace], position the cursor to the left of the letter "P" in the word "Practice."

5. PRESS: [BackSpace] *three times*
   The word "My" and the space are deleted. The text now reads "Practice Paragraph" once again.

6. To move the cursor down two lines without moving the text:
   PRESS: [End] *to move to the end of the line*
   PRESS: [Enter] *twice*
   The cursor is now in the correct position for you to begin typing the practice paragraph.

Quick Reference
Deleting Text

- Press Delete to delete text at the current cursor position.
- Press BackSpace to delete text to the left of the current cursor position.

UNDELETING TEXT

WordPerfect allows you to undelete text that has been previously deleted from your document. You can undelete text and insert it at the position of the cursor by choosing Edit, Undelete. The UNDELETE command lets you restore any or all of the last three deletions. The UNDELETE command differs from the UNDO command, in that Undelete restores the deleted text to the insertion point whereas Undo restores text to its original location. (Undo is discussed later in this session.) To practice using Undelete, perform the following steps:

1. Move to the top of the document:
   PRESS: Ctrl+Home

2. PRESS: Delete *three times*

3. PRESS: ↓ *two times*

4. CHOOSE: Edit, Undelete
   Notice that the three characters you deleted from the title, `Pra,` appear at the point of insertion. To restore this deletion, you would choose Restore. For the purposes of this exercise:
   CHOOSE: Cancel

5. To insert the deleted text in its original position:
   PRESS: Ctrl+Home
   TYPE: `Pra`

6. PRESS: End
   PRESS: Enter *twice*

WORD WRAP

The word wrap feature of WordPerfect allows you to continuously type without worrying about pressing Enter at the end of each line. If you are used to working on a typewriter, resist the temptation to hit a carriage return when the right margin approaches. In this section, you complete the original practice paragraph.

1. TYPE: `For some people the concept of writing using a computer is difficult to grasp. These people are accustomed to using the traditional tools for word processing -- pen, pencil, and paper, or a typewriter. It's natural to think that a new way of doing things is going to be difficult. However, once you have worked through this session, you'll wonder how you ever managed without a computer.`

2. PRESS: **Enter**
   Your screen should now appear similar to Figure 1.6.

Quick Reference
Word Wrap

When typing a paragraph, do not press **Enter** at the end of each line. **Enter** is used only to end a paragraph or to insert a blank line in a document.

USING THE UNDO AND REDO COMMANDS

The **UNDO command** allows you to cancel the last command you performed in a document. To undo an action, select the Edit option from the menu and then choose the Undo option or click on the Undo button () in the Toolbar. Unfortunately, the UNDO command works only for the last command performed, so make sure that you perform Undo *immediately* after making an error.

The **REDO command** reverses the last UNDO command. Like the UNDO option, REDO only cancels the last UNDO command that you issued. Click on the Redo button ().

To practice using the UNDO command, perform the following steps.

1. Make sure that you are in Insert mode ("Typeover" should *not* appear in the Status bar) and then insert another blank line at the bottom of the document you entered in the last section:
   PRESS: Enter

2. Type the following text in; don't correct any mistakes you might make while typing:
   TYPE: `This is a test of the UNDO command.`

3. To practice using the UNDO command:
   PRESS: BackSpace *eight times to delete the word "command"*
   CHOOSE: Edit, Undo
   The text you previously deleted should be displaying again in the document.

4. The cursor should be positioned to the right of "command."
   PRESS: BackSpace *until the sentence is deleted*

Note: The UNDO command doesn't always work. For example, you cannot undo an action that doesn't affect your document, such as scrolling.

Quick Reference
The UNDO Command

- CHOOSE: Edit, Undo from the Menu bar, or
- PRESS: Ctrl+z, or
- CLICK: Undo button in the Toolbar

GETTING HELP

WordPerfect provides context-sensitive Help when you press F1. *Context-sensitive* refers to WordPerfect's ability to retrieve Help information reflecting your current position in the program and your current needs. For other Help, you can use the Help option on the Menu bar; its commands are listed in Table 1.4.

Table 1.4 The Help Menu		
	Contents	A list of all the Help sections.
	Search for Help On	An index that helps you search for a specific topic.
	How Do I...	Help on performing common tasks such as editing, formatting, and saving.
	Macros	An on-line macros manual.
	Coaches	A list of mini-tutorials that coach you through a feature as you are using it.
	Upgrade Expert	Assists is moving from other word processing applications to WordPerfect 6.1
	Tutorial	A guided tour of WordPerfect basics.
	About WordPerfect	Product and license information about the memory status and version.

Perform the following steps to access the Help facility (Figure 1.7) through the Menu bar.

1. Choose the Help, Contents command from the menu:
   CHOOSE: Help, Contents

2. To move through the subject areas:
   PRESS: Tab *and* Shift+Tab

3. Position the mouse pointer over the subject areas but do not click the mouse button. Notice that the mouse pointer becomes a hand when moving over the topic areas.

4. To view Additional Help information about the menu commands (the fourth option listed on the screen), move the mouse pointer over the topic and click the left mouse button:
   CLICK: "Additional Help" topic
   An additional window, titled Indexes, now appears on the left-side of your screen, next to the WordPerfect Help window.

5. To highlight the first menu option:
   PRESS: **Tab** *twice*
   The cursor should now be highlighting the What's New option.
   PRESS: **Tab** *until the Print Topics option is highlighted*
   PRESS: **Enter** *to display information about the Print Topics option*

6. After reviewing the Help information, close the Indexes window:
   DOUBLE-CLICK: *the Indexes control menu (▬), located in the upper left corner of the Indexes screen*

7. Close the WordPerfect Help window:
   CHOOSE: File, Exit *from the WordPerfect Help window*
   (*Note*: Do not choose File Exit from the Document window!)

Perform the following steps to access context-sensitive help.

1. To access Help from anywhere in the program:
   PRESS: **F1**

2. After reading the Help information, close the window:
   CHOOSE: File, Exit

Figure 1.7

The Help facility

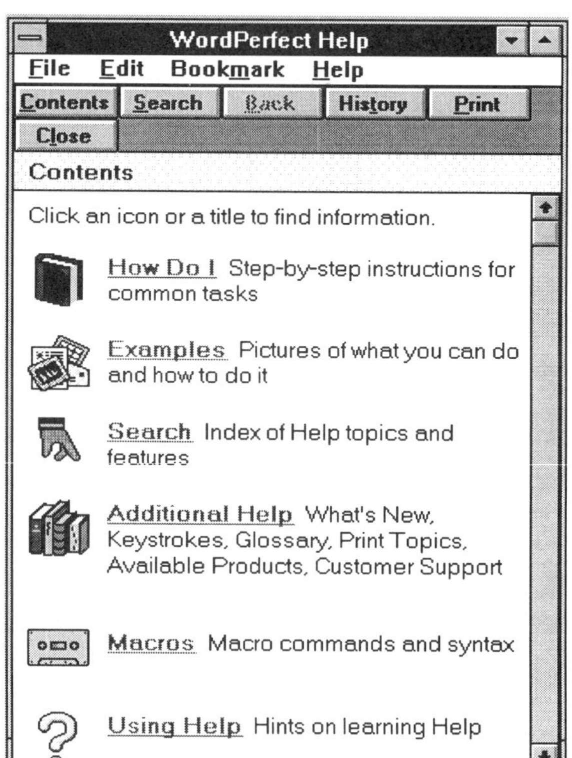

Perform the following steps to access context-sensitive Help for the menu commands:

1. To obtain the question mark mouse pointer for retrieving context-sensitive Help:
   PRESS: **Shift**+**F1**

2. To display Help for the File, Open command, use the question mark mouse pointer to access the command from the Menu bar:
   CHOOSE: File
   Click the left mouse button once on the word File in the menu.
   PRESS: **Tab** *two times to highlight the Open option and then press* **Enter**, *or highlight the option with the mouse pointer and then click the left mouse button*

3. After reading the Help information, close the window:
   CHOOSE: File, Exit

Quick Reference
Using Help

- Press **F1** to display context-sensitive Help.
- To display context-sensitive Help for a menu command, press **Shift**+**F1** to change the mouse pointer to a question mark, and select the menu command.
- To exit the Help facility, choose File, Exit.

SAVING AND CLOSING A DOCUMENT

SAVING A DOCUMENT

When you create or edit a document, you are working in the computer's RAM (random access memory). However, RAM is volatile, meaning that if you exit the word processing program or turn off the computer, you will lose your document. Therefore, you must save your work to a floppy diskette or hard disk for permanent storage before you exit or turn off the power.

To save a document to a disk, select the File, Save command or the File, Save As command from the Menu bar. Type in a filename of up to eight characters with no spaces, and then press **Enter** or choose Save. When completed, the filename is displayed in the Title bar, followed by the word "unmodified." WordPerfect is indicating that the file hasn't been modified since it was last saved. Once you make changes to the document, the "unmodified" designation will disappear.

Perform the following steps to use File, Save As to save the current document under the filename PRACTICE onto the Advantage Diskette.

1. Make sure that the Advantage Diskette is placed into drive A: or drive B:.

2. CHOOSE: File, Save As
   The File, Save and File, Save As commands are identical if the document has never been saved before. If a document has been previously saved, use the Save command to save modifications over the existing version. Use the Save As command to specify a new filename or a different disk drive for saving a file.

3. Depending on where the Advantage Diskette is located, type the following disk drive and filename:
   TYPE: `a:practice` or `b:practice`
   PRESS: **Enter** or CLICK: OK
   Notice that the drive letter is placed before the filename to ensure that the file is saved onto the Advantage Diskette. *Note*: Until you exit WordPerfect or specify a different disk drive, WordPerfect will temporarily change the default disk drive to the drive you specify when saving or opening a file.

WordPerfect adds the extension of WPD to all of your filenames. A file named PRACTICE.WPD is now stored on the Advantage Diskette.

Quick Reference
Saving a File

1. CHOOSE: File, Save As, or
   PRESS: **F3**
2. Type in the filename, including the drive letter.
3. Press **Enter** or CLICK: OK

When working on an important document, you should save the document every 15 to 20 minutes to protect it against a power outage or other catastrophe that shuts down your computer. The FILE SAVE command replaces the existing file on the disk with the version that you are currently working on in memory; if your objective is to replace the file on disk with the contents of memory, the FILE SAVE command is faster than choosing File, Save As.

WordPerfect for Windows provides a few quick methods for saving a document to the disk. Using a mouse, select the Save icon in the Toolbar.

Even though you haven't made any changes to the PRACTICE document, use the following command to see how it works:

CLICK: [Save icon] *on the Toolbar*

The PRACTICE document has again been saved onto the Advantage Diskette.

Quick Reference
Saving a File Under the Same Name

This command replaces an old version of a file with a new version of the file.

- CHOOSE: File, Save, or
- PRESS: Ctrl+S, or
- CLICK: Save icon on the Toolbar [Save icon]

Sometimes it is necessary to save a new version of a previously saved document under a different name. For example, you may want to keep all the different versions of a document on file to see how the document developed over time. After you create a document once, you can use that document as a template for future documents that are similar. Rather than retyping the new document, you can retrieve the old file, fill in the new information, and then save it under a different name by choosing File, Save As.

CLOSING A DOCUMENT

When you are finished working with a document, you should close the file to free up RAM space. To close a document, choose File, Close from the Menu bar. If there are no other documents open, the Document area will be empty.

Let's close the PRACTICE document file.

1. CHOOSE: File, Close
   Your screen should look like it did when you first loaded WordPerfect.

2. If there are other documents appearing in the Document area, repeat step 1 to clear them from memory. When finished, your screen should look like it did when you first loaded WordPerfect.

Quick Reference
Closing a Document

CHOOSE: File, Close

OPENING AN EXISTING DOCUMENT

You store and manage documents on diskettes or the hard disk. To modify or print an existing document, you must first retrieve the file from storage by choosing File, Open, or pressing Ctrl+O, or clicking the Open icon ( ) in the Power bar. Once the Open dialog box is displayed, you will perform the following procedure:

> If you are using a mouse, select the appropriate options from the Drives and Filename list boxes. For example, to retrieve a file named BUDGET off the Advantage Diskette in drive B:, double-click on b: in the Drives list box and then click on the name BUDGET in the Filename list box (you may have to use the scroll button to see additional files in the Filename list box). Then click OK.

Perform the following steps to retrieve the PRACTICE document from the Advantage Diskette:

1. Make sure that the Advantage Diskette is placed into either drive A: or drive B:.

2. CHOOSE: File, Open
   The Open File dialog box is displayed (Figure 1.8). *Note*: The files in Figure 1.8 may be different than the ones you are viewing.

Figure 1.8

The Open File dialog box

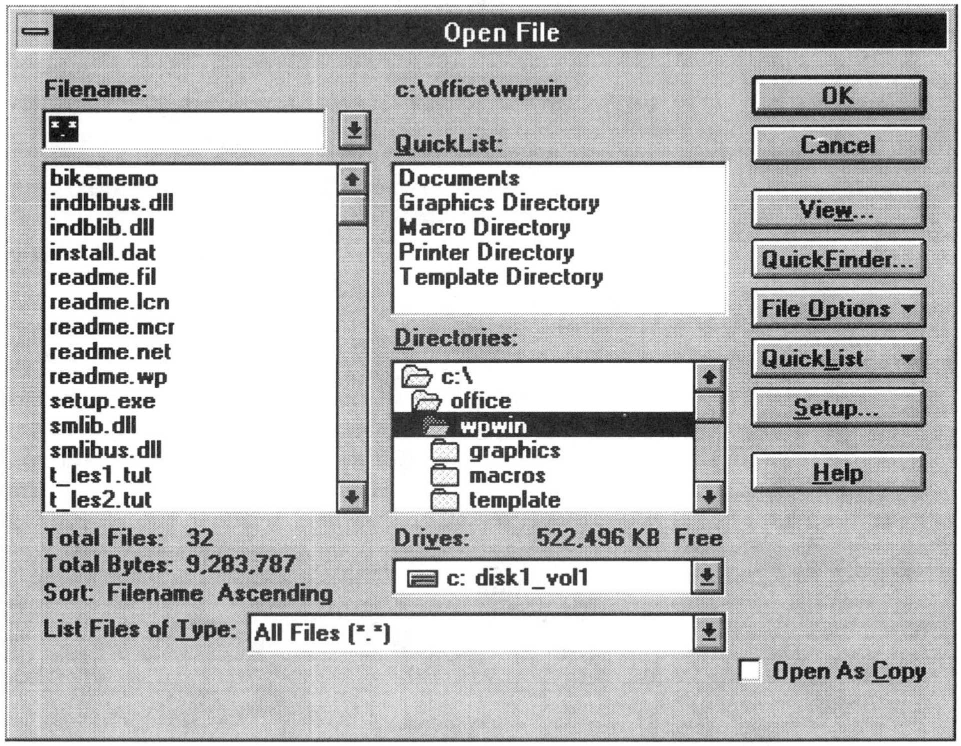

3. To list the files on the Advantage Diskette:
   CLICK: in the Drives list box
   CLICK: A: or B: *depending on where the Advantage Diskette is located*

4. Choose PRACTICE from the Filename list box by selecting it with the mouse and then clicking OK, or by double-clicking on PRACTICE. *Note*: You may need to drag the scroll button before you can see the PRACTICE file on the screen.

   The document is retrieved from the disk and displayed on the screen.

Quick Reference
Opening a Document

1. CHOOSE: File, Open, or
   CLICK: Open button ( )
2. Select the appropriate options from the Drives and Filename list boxes. Once you select a file in the Filename list box, click OK.

BEGINNING A NEW DOCUMENT

When WordPerfect is first loaded, a blank document area is automatically displayed on the screen. However, if you finish working on a document and want to start work on a new one, you must request a new document by choosing File, New, or clicking the New Document icon ().

Do the following to display a blank document:

1. CHOOSE: File, New
2. The "New Document" dialog box is displaying:

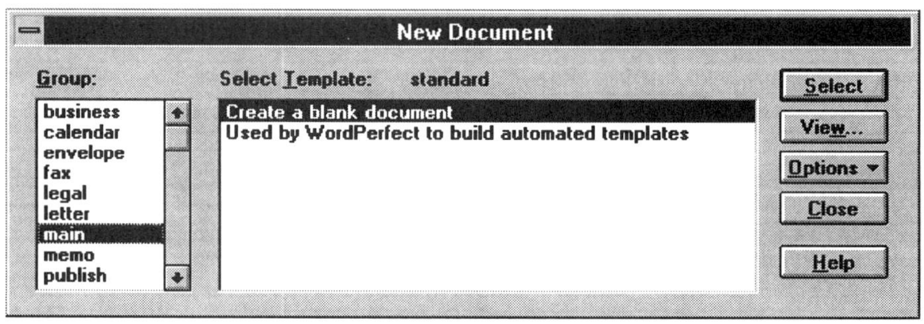

3. Notice the the "Create a blank document" option is selected in the "Select Template" area. To accept this assumption:
   CLICK: Select button or PRESS: **Enter**

Your screen should look like it did when you first loaded WordPerfect except that in the Title bar you see the text "Document2 - unmodified." At this point you would create and then save your new document using procedures described in this session.

Quick Reference *Creating a New Document*	CHOOSE: File, New, or PRESS: **Ctrl**+N, or CLICK: New Document icon ()

LEAVING WORDPERFECT FOR WINDOWS

When you are finished using WordPerfect, save your work and exit the program before turning off the computer. If you have made modifications to the document and have not saved the changes, WordPerfect asks whether the revisions should be saved or abandoned before exiting the program. In this session, you have already saved the document and have not made any modifications since retrieving it in the last section.

Perform the following steps to finish working with WordPerfect for Windows.

1. To exit WordPerfect for Windows:
   CHOOSE: File, Exit
   Assuming that no changes were made to the document, the application is closed and you are returned to the Program Manager.

2. To exit Windows:
   CHOOSE: File, Exit
   Note: Rather than using the menu commands, you can double-click the Application Control menu (▬) to close an application.
   Windows now asks if you really want to exit.
   CLICK: OK

Quick Reference
Exiting WordPerfect and Windows

1. CHOOSE: File, Exit or double-click WordPerfect's Application Control menu (▬)
2. CHOOSE: File, Exit or double-click the Program Manager's Application Control menu (▬)

SUMMARY

This session introduced you to working with word processing software programs, specifically WordPerfect 6.1 for Windows. We began the session exploring the advantages of computer-based word processing over typewriters. The session discussed loading Windows and WordPerfect and listed the program's major components, including the Program Manager, group icons, program icons, and Application and Document windows. WordPerfect's Help facility provided some assistance on menu commands.

In the latter half of the session, you created a practice document using the Insert and Typeover modes. You learned how to remove characters using Delete and BackSpace and how to use Enter to insert blank lines in the document. The session finished with discussions on saving, closing, and opening document files.

COMMAND SUMMARY

Many of the commands and procedures appearing in this session are provided in the command summary in Table 1.5.

Table 1.5

Command Summary

COMMAND	TASK
File, New	Create a new document file ( ).
File, Open	Open an existing (saved) document file ( ).
File, Close	Close a document file.
File, Save	Save a document to the disk using the same directory and filename ( ).
File, Save As	Save a document to the disk, specifying a new filename.
File, Exit	Leave WordPerfect for Windows.
Edit, Undo	Reverse the last command executed ( ).
Edit, Redo	Reverses the last UNDO command executed ( ).
F1	Display context-sensitive Help.

KEY TERMS

application window In Microsoft Windows, each running application program appears in its own Application window.

Clipboard A Microsoft Windows feature. To copy and move information within an application or among applications, you copy the information onto the Clipboard and paste it from the Clipboard to the new location.

cursor The vertical flashing bar in WordPerfect for Windows that indicates your current position in the document. The cursor shows where the next typed characters or spaces will appear or where command data will be entered.

dialog box A box that displays messages or asks for confirmation of commands.

document window In Microsoft Windows, each open document appears in its own Document window. These windows can be sized and moved anywhere within the document area. (A Document window represents your workspace.)

DOS Acronym for Disk Operating System. Internal command instructions for certain microcomputers.

grammar checker Software feature that allows the user to analyze punctuation, sentence structure, and word usage.

graphical user interface (GUI) Software feature that allows the user to select menu options and icons instead of remembering complicated command language; makes software easier to use and typically employs a mouse.

icon A picture or screen that represents a program or a software function.

Insert mode A mode of entering text. Insert mode allows the user to insert text at the current cursor position without typing over existing text. Existing text is pushed to the right.

mail merge A word processing procedure that typically involves combining data—such as names and addresses—that is stored in a data file with a form letter stored in a separate file.

Microsoft Windows Graphical user interface software that works with DOS to make it easier for users to run programs.

mouse Handheld input device connected to a microcomputer by a cable; when the mouse is rolled across the desktop, the cursor moves on the screen. A button on the mouse allows users to make menu selections and to issue commands.

multitasking Activity in which more than one task or program is executed at one time.

OLE Acronym for Microsoft Windows' Object Linking and Embedding technology. This feature of Windows programs facilitates the exchange of data between applications.

Program Manager The primary window or shell for Microsoft Windows. Applications are organized and launched from the Program Manager window.

REDO command In a software application, a command that reverses, or cancels, the last UNDO command executed.

spelling checker In word processing programs, a program that checks the spelling of words in a document.

thesaurus In word processing programs, a program that provides a list of synonyms for a currently selected word or phrase.

Typeover mode A mode of entering text. With Typeover mode, the newly typed text overwrites the existing text.

UNDO command In a software application, a command that reverses, or cancels, the last command executed.

word processing Preparation of a document using a microcomputer and software for creating, editing, formatting, and printing documents.

word wrap When the cursor reaches the right-hand margin of a line, it automatically wraps to the left margin of the next line; the user does not have to press a carriage return key at the end of each line.

WYSIWYG Acronym for What You See Is What You Get; page description software that allows the user to see the final version of a document on the screen—including the results of formatting—before it is printed out.

EXERCISES

SHORT ANSWER

1. Compared to using a typewriter, what are some of the advantages of using a word processing program?
2. List the advantages of working in the Microsoft Windows environment.
3. What are the four levels of formatting in a document?
4. What are some examples of mail merge activities?
5. Why is it significant to know that WordPerfect operates in Insert mode?

6. What is the procedure for exiting WordPerfect and then Windows?
7. What happens if you press Enter when the cursor is in the middle of a paragraph?
8. How do you delete a character or space to the left of the cursor?
9. What is meant by the term *word wrap*?
10. What is the difference between choosing File, Save and File, Save As?

HANDS-ON

(*Note*: In the following exercises, save your documents onto and retrieve files from the Advantage Diskette.)

1. Create the document appearing in Figure 1.9. Make sure you include your name and job title (real or imaginary) in the closing of the letter. Save this document onto the Advantage Diskette as WORDLTR. (*Note*: Additional steps follow on the next page.)

Figure 1.9

WORDLTR document

March 24, 1995

Mr. Al Martino
210 Spruce Way
Stanford, CA 94305

Dear Mr. Martino:

Thank you for your letter regarding the upcoming event. I am in complete agreement with you that the number of persons attending must be limited to 200. I like your idea of having this event catered.

Moving to a different subject, I noticed that the letter you wrote me was typed using a typewriter. (You certainly do use a lot of correction fluid!) With the number of letters you write, you really should consider purchasing a microcomputer and word processing software.

If you are interested, come over to my office, and I will show you some word processing fundamentals. We could even use my computer to design and print all of the invitations for the event!

Best regards,

your name

a. Insert the following text between the second and third paragraphs (make sure you insert a line of space above and below the inserted text):

Specifically, word processing software makes it easier to change a document by allowing you to:

1. Insert text
2. Move text

```
3.    Copy text
4.    Delete text
```

b. In the first line of the last paragraph, delete the words "If you are interested," and start the sentence with "You should."

c. In the second paragraph, replace the phrase "correction fluid" with "white out" using Typeover mode and **Delete**.

d. Save the document back to the Advantage Diskette as WORDLTR. Replace the existing version of the file.

e. Close the WORDLTR document.

2. Create the document appearing in Figure 1.10. Make sure you include your name in the closing of the letter. Save this document onto the Advantage Diskette as ABCLTR.

   a. In the second paragraph, perform the following editing changes:

Text Before Editing	Text After Editing
`DOS 3.3`	`Microsoft DOS 6.2`
`Windows 3.0`	`Microsoft Windows 3.1`
`at that time`	`the next morning`

   b. Remove the entire third paragraph, starting with "Training on."

   c. Enter the phone number (800)581-8799 below the last line.

   d. Save the document as ABCLTR onto the Advantage Diskette.

   e. Close the document.

   f. Open ABCLTR document from the Advantage Diskette.

   g. Edit the phone number to read (800)588-1799.

   h. Save and close the document once again.

Figure 1.10

ABCLTR document

June 28, 1995

Mr. S. Luis Obispo
Manager, Sales
ABC Realty Inc.
1388 Primrose Lane
Albany, GA 31705

Dear Luis:

Per our discussion yesterday, please accept this letter as confirmation of your order for computer equipment, deliverable next week.

As ordered, five computers will be installed: one at reception, two for sales, one for accounting, and the last one for yourself. We will also be installing DOS 3.3, Windows 3.0, and WordPerfect for Windows 6.1 at that time.

Training on these software programs will begin the week after installation, per the schedule arranged in our meeting. The cost of the training is included in the total cost of the equipment.

If I can be of any further assistance before the installation, or if you have any questions, please do not hesitate to contact me.

Yours sincerely,
Tech Talk Technology

your name
Accounts Representative

3. Write a one- to two-page document summarizing the useful features of word processing software. Include your name and the current date in the document. Save this letter onto the Advantage Diskette as FEATURES.

SESSION 2

WORDPERFECT 6.1 FOR WINDOWS: FORMATTING COMMANDS

Word processing programs include default values or assumptions that determine how a document appears when printed. For most business documents, these default settings work well. However, on occasion, you may need to use formatting commands to tailor documents to meet your specific needs.

PREVIEW

When you have completed this session, you will be able to:

Move efficiently through a document

•

Select text in a document for formatting

•

Delete blocks of text

•

Use character formatting commands to:
change typefaces and font sizes
boldface, italicize, and underline text

•

Use paragraph formatting commands to:
indent paragraphs
align or justify text
change line spacing
set tab stops

•

Print a document

Session Outline

WHY IS THIS SESSION IMPORTANT?

In this session you learn how to change WordPerfect's formatting assumptions, or default settings. These settings affect how your documents appear on the screen and how they look when printed. Not only do formatting commands enable you to customize your work; they also provide you with the tools for emphasizing points and improving the general readability of documents.

This session introduces the most commonly used character and paragraph formatting commands. The objective is to customize documents for printing.

Before proceeding, make sure the following are true:

1. You have loaded WordPerfect 6.1 for Windows.
2. You have an empty document area displayed.
3. Your Advantage Diskette is inserted into drive A: or drive B:. You will save your work onto the diskette and retrieve files that have been created for you. (*Note*: The Advantage Diskette can be duplicated by copying all the files from your instructor's Master Advantage Diskette.)

WORDPERFECT'S DEFAULT SETTINGS

When you first load WordPerfect for Windows, WordPerfect makes certain formatting assumptions that remain in effect unless you change them; these **default settings**, or assumptions, are shown in Table 2.1.

Before practicing the formatting commands, you will learn how to move the cursor efficiently through a document.

Table 2.1

WordPerfect 6.1 for Windows Formatting Assumptions

Page Size	8.5" wide by 11" long
Top and Bottom Margins	1"
Left and Right Margins	1"
Page Numbering	None
Line Spacing	Single-space
Font	Times New Roman, 12 point
Tabs	Every 1/2"
Text Justification	Left justified (aligned) with a ragged right margin (text is not aligned on the right)

MOVING THE CURSOR

There are better ways to move around a document than pressing the cursor-movement keys. Although these keys worked well in the previous exercises, they do not provide the most efficient methods for moving through longer documents. This section introduces the keyboard shortcuts, summarized in Table 2.2, for moving the cursor through a document.

Perform the following steps to open a document named ETHICS, and then practice moving through a document.

1. Make sure that the Advantage Diskette is inserted into drive A: or drive B:.

2. Open the document that you will use to practice the cursor-movement commands:
   CHOOSE: File, Open
   CLICK: a: or b: (if necessary) *in the Drives list box*
   SELECT: ETHICS.WPD *in the Filename list box*
   (*Note*: You may need to drag the scroll button before you can see the ETHICS filename on the screen.)
   PRESS: Enter or CLICK: OK

Table 2.2

Cursor-Movement Commands

Keys	Action
↑ or ↓	Move the cursor up or down one line.
Ctrl+↑	Move the cursor to the previous paragraph.
Ctrl+↓	Move the cursor to the next paragraph.
← or →	Move the cursor to the previous or next character.
Ctrl+←	Move the cursor to the beginning of the previous word.
Ctrl+→	Move the cursor to the beginning of the next word.
PgUp	Move the cursor up one screen.
PgDn	Move the cursor down one screen.
Home	Move to the beginning of the current line (before codes)
Home, Home	Move to the beginning of the current line.
End	Move to the end of the current line.
Ctrl+Home	Move to the beginning of the document (cursor in front of text).
Ctrl+Home, Ctrl+Home	Move to the beginning of the document (cursor in front of codes *and* text).
Ctrl+End	Move to the end of the document.

Your screen should now appear similar to Figure 2.1.

Note: From now on in this guide, we will instruct you to open a file without providing the specific steps for opening. If necessary, refer to Session 1 to review opening files.

Figure 2.1

The ETHICS.WPD document

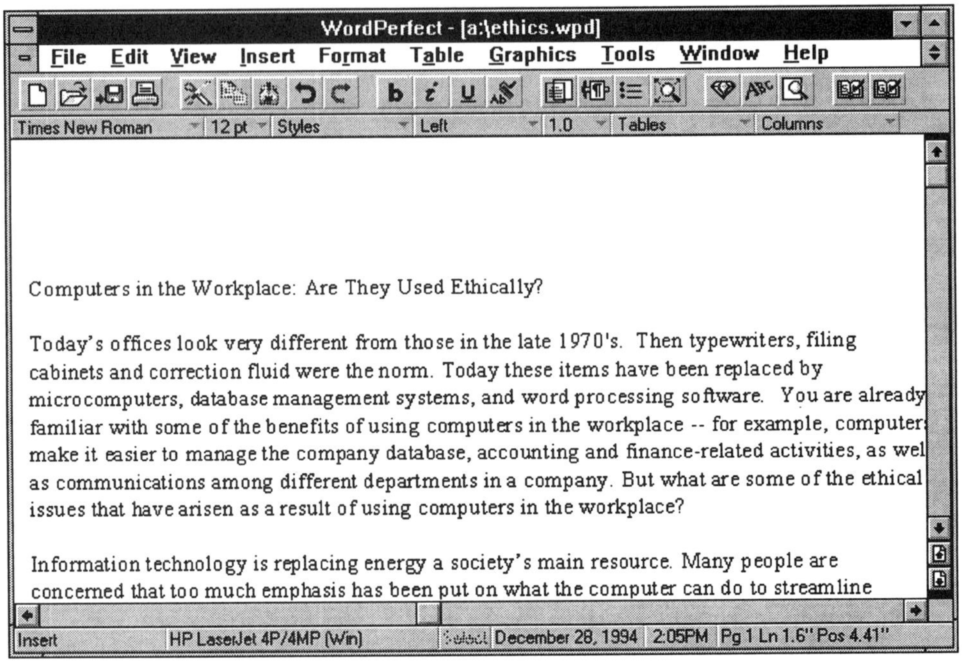

5. Move to the bottom of the document:
   PRESS: Ctrl+End
   Note the page and line numbers on the Status bar.

6. Move back to the top of the document:
   PRESS: Ctrl+Home

7. Move to the end of the current line:
   PRESS: End

8. Move to the beginning of the current line:
   PRESS: Home

9. Move to the beginning of the first paragraph:
   PRESS: ↓ *twice*

10. Move to the fourth word in the first sentence:
    PRESS: Ctrl+→ *three times*

11. Move back to the second word in the current line:
    PRESS: Ctrl+← *twice*

12. To move to the top of the second page in the document:
    CHOOSE: Edit, Go To
    TYPE: 2
    PRESS: Enter or CLICK: OK
    The cursor automatically moved to the first line of the second page.

13. To move to the top of the document:
    PRESS: Ctrl+Home

Quick Reference
The GOTO Command

To move the cursor to a specific page in a document, choose Edit, Go To. Then type in the page number and press Enter.

SELECTING TEXT

Once text has been typed into a document, formatting changes are made by first selecting the text, using the keyboard or mouse, and then issuing the appropriate formatting command. Selected text always appears highlighted in reverse video. In other words, selected text appears white on black if your video display is normally black on white. A selection may comprise letters, words, lines, paragraphs, or the entire document. When you finish formatting a selection, press a cursor-movement key or click anywhere in the document to remove the highlighting from the text.

BLOCKING TEXT

Methods for selecting a word, sentence, paragraph, or the entire document using the mouse are summarized in Table 2.3. To extend the selection to include several words, lines, or paragraphs, make the initial selection and then hold down the left mouse button and drag the pointer over the desired text.

To practice selecting text using a mouse, perform the following steps.

1. To select the word "Computers" in the title of the document on your screen, first position the I-beam mouse pointer over the word.

2. DOUBLE-CLICK: "Computers"
   The word and the following space should be highlighted. If the word isn't highlighted, keep trying to double-click the mouse button with the I-beam over the word "Computers."

Table 2.3

Selecting Text Using the Mouse

Single Letter	Position the I-beam pointer to the left of the letter you want to select. Press down and hold the left mouse button as you drag the mouse pointer to the right.
Single Word	Position the I-beam pointer on the word and double-click the left mouse button.
Single Sentence	Position the I-beam pointer on the sentence and click the left mouse button three times.
Block of Text	Move the cursor to the beginning of the block of text, and then position the mouse pointer I-beam at the end of the block. Hold down **Shift** and click once. *Note*: Use this method to highlight the entire document.
Single Paragraph	Position the I-beam pointer on the paragraph and click the left mouse button four times.

3. To select the letters "Work" of the word "Workplace," first move the mouse pointer I-beam to the left of the "W" in "Workplace."

4. PRESS: *left mouse button and hold down*
   DRAG: *I-beam to the right until the word "Work" is highlighted and then let go of the mouse button*

5. To select the first sentence in the first paragraph below the title, first position the I-beam mouse pointer over any word in the sentence.

6. CLICK: *left mouse button three times*
   The first sentence, including the period and following space, is highlighted.

7. To select the entire first paragraph, position the I-beam mouse pointer or the cursor somewhere in the first paragraph.

8. CLICK: *left mouse button four times*
   The first paragraph, including the period and any blank lines, is highlighted.

9. To select the entire document:
   CHOOSE: Edit, Select, All

10. CLICK: *anywhere in the text area*
    The highlighting should be removed.

11. PRESS: **Ctrl**+**Home**

Methods for using the keyboard to select a word, line, paragraph, or the entire document are summarized in Table 2.4.

Table 2.4

Selecting Text Using the Keyboard

Single Letter	Position the cursor to the left of the letter you want to select. Press **Shift**+**→**.
Single Word	Position the cursor in the word you want to select, and then hold down **Shift** and press **Ctrl**+**→**.
Sentence	Position the cursor in the sentence you want to select, and then choose Edit, Select, Sentence.
Paragraph	Position the cursor in the paragraph you want to select, and then choose Edit, Select, Paragraph.
Page	Position the cursor in the page you want to select, and then choose Edit, Select, Page.
Entire Document (All)	Position the cursor anywhere in the document, and then choose Edit, Select, All.

DELETING BLOCKS OF TEXT

You previously deleted one character at a time using BackSpace and Delete. You can also press Ctrl+BackSpace to delete the word that is nearest to the cursor. Using this procedure, the cursor must be one character to the left or right of the word to be deleted. However, selecting text allows you to easily perform editing procedures on larger blocks of text.

Perform the following steps to practice deleting and replacing text in a document.

1. SELECT: the text "Are They Used Ethically?" (*in the title*)

2. To remove this phrase from the title:
   PRESS: Delete

3. Press BackSpace to delete the colon (:) that is currently displaying as the last character in the title.

4. Move the mouse pointer I-beam over the word "Computers."
   DOUBLE-CLICK: "Computers"
   Only the word has been selected.

5. TYPE: `Technology`
   As you can see, rather than using the Typeover mode, you can select the text to be replaced and type in the new information. The typing automatically replaces the text selection and WordPerfect adjusts the spacing.

6. To bring "Computers" back into the title:
   DOUBLE-CLICK: "Technology"
   TYPE: `Computers`

7. Close the document and do not save the changes:
   CHOOSE: File, Close
   SELECT: No *when asked if you want to save your changes*

Now that you know how to move through documents and select text using the mouse and keyboard, you will find it easy to use the formatting commands. The next section begins with an introduction to the character formatting commands.

CHARACTER FORMATTING COMMANDS

In WordPerfect for Windows, enhancing text is referred to as *character formatting*. Specifically, character formatting involves selecting typefaces, type sizes, and styles for text. Some of the styles available in WordPerfect include bold, italic, underline, strikethrough, superscript, and subscript. Although these enhancement features are effective in drawing attention to text, they can also detract from the message of a document. Some publishing professionals advocate four typefaces or fonts as the maximum for any one document. Still, there is no better guage than common sense and good taste!

WordPerfect's character formatting commands are accessed through the Format, Font command (Figure 2.2), the Toolbar, or by using shortcut keyboard combinations. Since the most common features are accessible from the Toolbar and Power bar, you may never need to access the menu except to see a preview of the desired font in the dialog box. Table 2.5 summarizes the mouse and keyboard methods for choosing character formatting commands after you have selected the desired text.

Figure 2.2

The Font dialog box

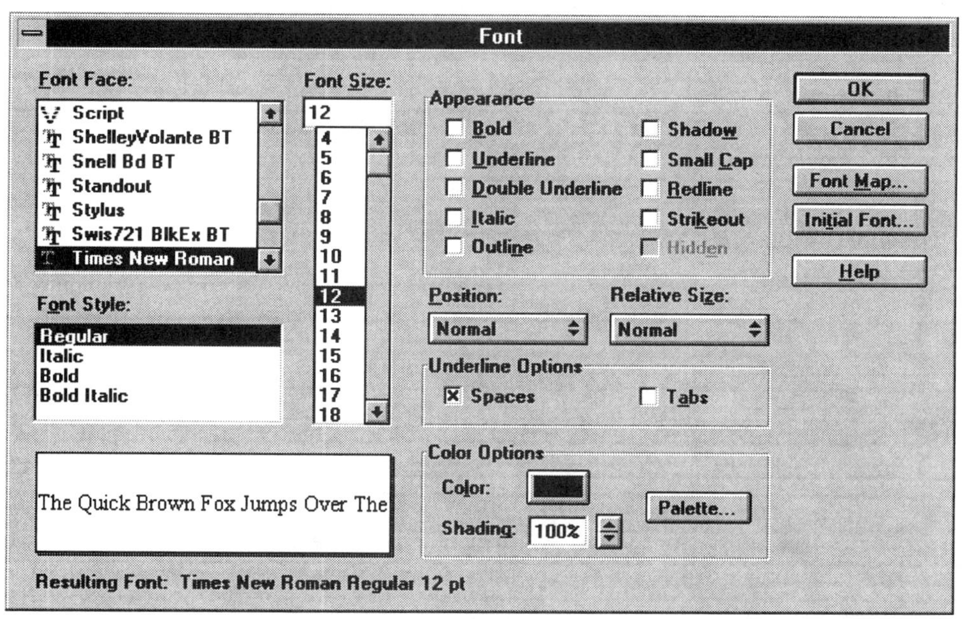

Table 2.5

Character Formatting Summary

Toolbar or Power bar button	*Keyboard Shortcut*	*Description*
b	Ctrl+b	Makes the selected text **bold**
i	Ctrl+i	*Italicizes* the selected text
u	Ctrl+u	Underlines the selected text
Times New Roman		Specifies a font or typeface
12 pt		Specifies a point size for the font

BOLDFACE, ITALIC, AND UNDERLINE

WordPerfect allows you to apply character formatting commands as you type or after you have selected text. Perform the following steps to apply boldface, italic, and underlines to the ETHICS document.

1. Open the ETHICS document from the Advantage Diskette. (*Note*: The last four documents that you've opened are listed at the bottom of the File pull-down menu. Choose the ETHICS file from this list.)

2. Insert a new line between the title and the first paragraph:
   PRESS: End
   PRESS: Enter

3. To add a subtitle to this document and italicize it as you're typing it in:
   PRESS: Ctrl+i

4. TYPE: `The Information Age and the Age of Humanity`

5. To stop typing in italic:
   PRESS: Ctrl+i

6. To select this subtitle, position the mouse pointer in the blank space to the left of the subtitle. This area is called the Selection area. Click the left mouse button once to select the subtitle text.

7. To make the subtitle appear bold:
   CLICK: Bold button (b)

8. To make the subtitle appear underlined:
   CLICK: Underline button (u)

9. To remove the highlighting:
   CLICK: *anywhere in the text area*

10. Perform the following formatting changes to the text in the first paragraph:

Text to Be Formatted	*Format Type*
`microcomputers`	italic and bold
`database management systems`	italic
`word processing software`	italic
`ethical issues`	underline

Quick Reference
Boldface, Italic, and Underline

- To make text bold, press Ctrl+b or click the Bold button (b).
- To italicize text, press Ctrl+i or click the Italic button (i).
- To underline text, press Ctrl+u or click the Underline button (u).

TYPEFACES, FONTS, AND POINT SIZES

Some of the more interesting character formatting tasks include selecting typefaces to use in a document. A **typeface** is a style of print, whereas a **font** is defined as all the symbols and characters of a particular typeface for a given point size. Many DOS word processing programs do not utilize a variety of fonts, unless they are available through an individual software vendor or resident in the printer's memory. Microsoft Windows, on the other hand, provides easy access to several different typefaces.

The font and point size can be changed before typing new text or after selecting text. Although you can access the Font dialog box by choosing Format, Font to set the font and point size, it is easier to use the drop-down lists on the Power bar. Perform the following steps to change some of the fonts and point sizes in the ETHICS document.

1. SELECT: the main title *located on the first line*

2. To display a list of the available fonts:
   CLICK: down arrow next to the Font Face button (Times New Roman)

3. Scroll through the font choices by clicking the up and down arrows on the drop-down list's scroll bar or by dragging the scroll box.

   Note: If only a few Courier fonts are displaying on the screen, ask your instructor or lab assistant to help you install a Windows printer so you will have additional fonts.

4. SELECT: Arial
   You select a font from a drop-down list by clicking on it.

5. To display the range of available font sizes:
   CLICK: down arrow next to the Font Size drop-down list (12 pt)

6. SELECT: 16-point font size
   CLICK: Bold button (**b**)
   PRESS: **Home** *to remove the highlighting*
   The ETHICS document should look similar to Figure 2.3.

Figure 2.3

The ETHICS.WPD document after character formatting

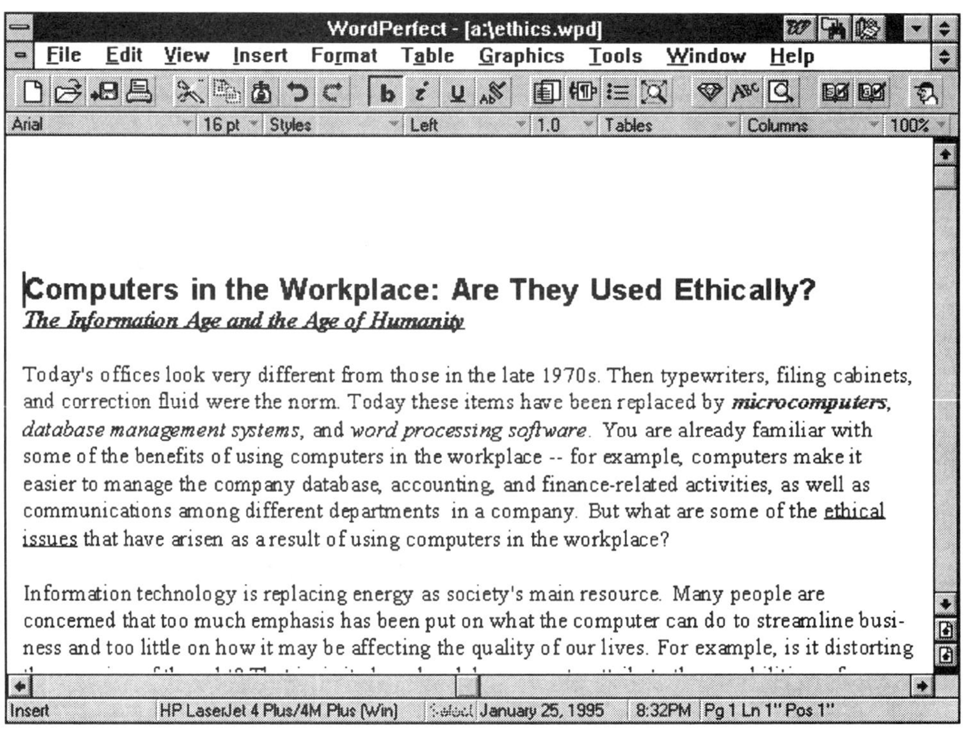

7. Save the document to the Advantage Diskette as ETHICS1 by choosing File, Save As. Refer to Session 1 if you need help saving the document.

8. Close the document.
   CHOOSE: File, Close

In the next section you learn how to reveal the codes WordPerfect inserts in your documents. This procedure is especially helpful when you are using WordPerfect's paragraph formatting commands (you'll use these shortly).

Quick Reference
Typefaces, Fonts, and Point Sizes

- To select a typeface, click the Font Face drop-down list (Times New Roman) in the Power bar and then click the desired font.
- To change the font size, click the Font Size drop-down list (12 pt) in the Power bar and then click the desired point size.

REVEAL CODES

When you type characters such as the letters A through Z, they appear on the screen. However, WordPerfect embeds some "invisible" characters, or codes, into the document as you're working on it. Revealing these invisible codes—that is, making them visible—can be quite helpful, especially after you've pressed a few keys accidentally and discover that some of your editing functions don't work because you've inadvertently inserted an unwanted code. Once the embedded codes are revealed, you can delete an unwanted code by positioning the cursor on it and pressing **Delete**. You choose View, Reveal Codes, or press **Alt**+**F3** to reveal the codes in a document.

Perform the following steps to practice revealing codes:

1. Open the WPTEMP document from the Advantage Diskette. If necessary, refer to Session 1 if you need help retrieving (opening) a document. (*Note*: You may have to scroll down to see additional files.)

2. The cursor should be at the top of the document. To reveal the codes:
   CHOOSE: View, Reveal Codes, *or*
   PRESS: Alt+F3
   The screen should look similar to Figure 2.4.

3. Many people find the display in Figure 2.4 confusing. The top part of the screen displays the document without the embedded codes, and the bottom part of the screen displays the document with the embedded codes revealed. When the cursor is moved through the document, it is simultaneously moved through both the top and bottom document screens. The SRt (soft return) codes at the end of many of the lines are WordPerfect's way of symbolizing word wrap. A HRt (hard return) code at the end of a paragraph means Enter was pressed. Table 2.6 includes a partial list of the codes that WordPerfect embeds in your documents.

Figure 2.4

Revealing codes

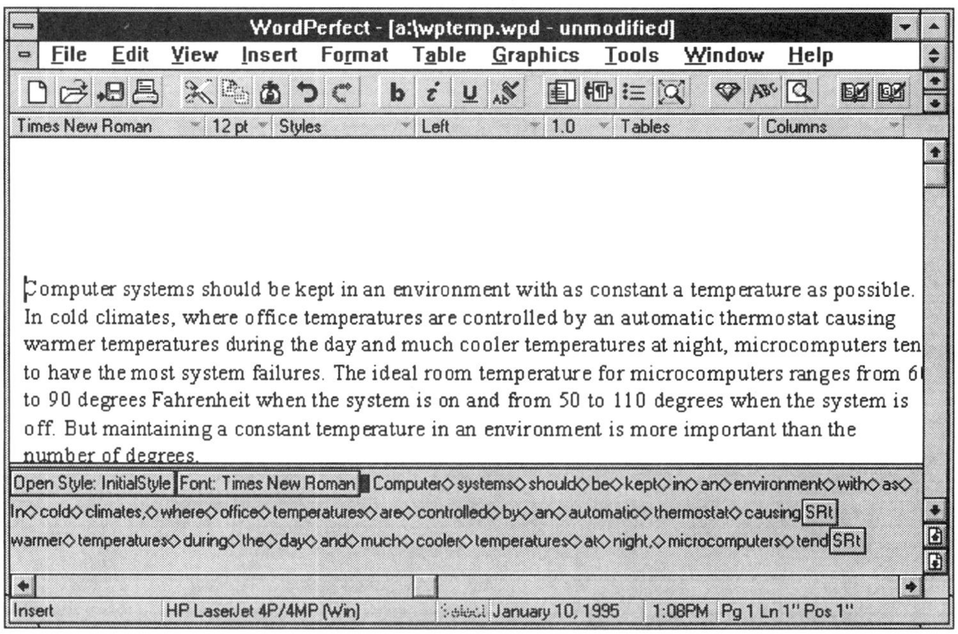

4. Practice moving the cursor to see the cursor, or highlight, move in the bottom part of the screen.

5. To turn the REVEAL CODES command off:
   CHOOSE: View, Reveal Codes, *or*
   PRESS: Alt+F3

PARAGRAPH FORMATTING COMMANDS

Paragraph formatting involves changing indents, alignment, justification, line spacing, and tab settings. When using a paragraph formatting command, you can format a portion of the document by selecting the text first and then using the appropriate formatting command. Or, you can format the rest of the document by positioning the cursor where you want the format change to begin taking effect and then using the appropriate formatting command. In the latter case, your document is affected from the current cursor position downward.

Table 2.6

Partial List of Embedded Codes

CODE	DESCRIPTION
[Bold]	Bold text attribute
[Header A]	Header A Definition
[Footer B]	Footer B Definition
[HPg]	Hard page break (inserted by the user)
[HRt]	Hard return inserted by pressing **Enter**
[Just]	Justification
[Lft Mar]	Left margin code
[Ln Spacing]	Line spacing
[Pg Num Pos]	Position of page number
[Rgt Mar]	Right margin code
[SRt]	Soft return
[Tab Set]	Tab set
[Und]	Underline text attribute

Many paragraph formatting commands are accessible from the Format menu. Some of the more popular features also work from the Ruler bar, which we will show you how to display in the next section. Using a mouse, you can easily set tab stops and even change the margins by dragging symbols on the Ruler bar. Using the keyboard, choose options from the Format menu.

DISPLAYING THE RULER BAR

Perform the following steps to display the Ruler and the Power and Toolbars:

1. The WPTEMP document should be displaying on the screen.

2. To display the Ruler and Toolbar:
   CHOOSE: View, Ruler Bar
   The screen should look like Figure 2.5. In the next section the Ruler bar will serve as a reference while you indent paragraphs using the Format menu. Then we will lead you through using the Ruler bar to perform paragraph formatting commands.

Figure 2.5

The Ruler, Toolbar and Power bar are displaying.

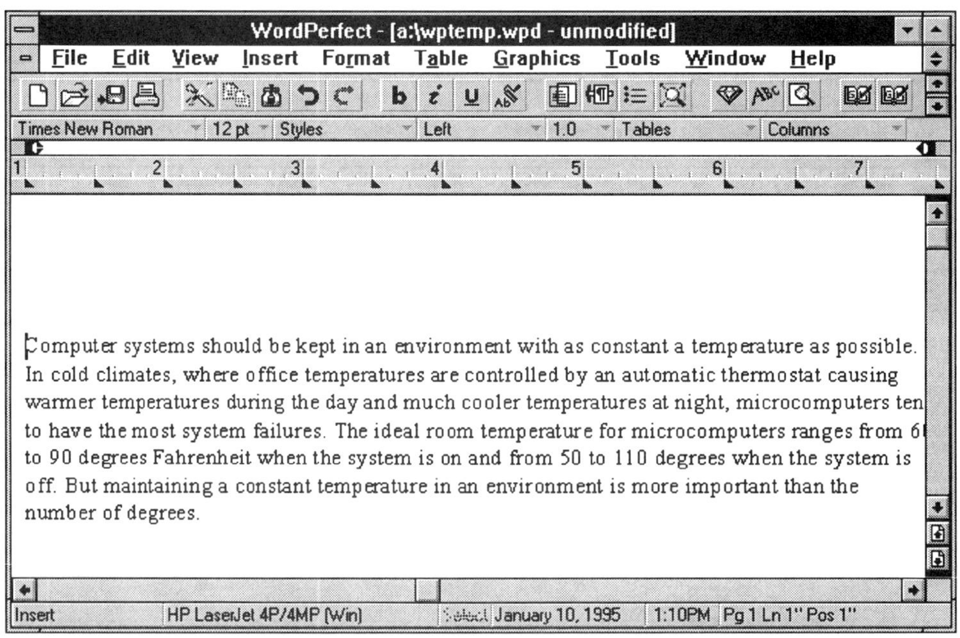

INDENTING PARAGRAPHS

Indenting text is similar to changing a left or right margin, except that indent codes don't affect the entire document (you learn how to change margins in Session 4). Think of an indent code as a temporary margin change, because indent codes affect only paragraphs; that is, text conforms to the indent code until the Enter code (HRt) is encountered in the document. If a document needs a variety of margin changes, it may be easier to indent. WordPerfect allows you to indent on the left margin or on both margins by choosing Format, Paragraph.

WordPerfect provides five different types of indents for changing the appearance of a paragraph:

- *Standard Paragraph Indent*
  To indent the first line of a paragraph, position the cursor at the beginning of the paragraph and press Tab. The first line will be indented to the next tab stop. The [Tab] code is inserted in your document.

- *Indent* (F7)
  To move the entire body of a paragraph in from the left margin, choose Format, Paragraph, Indent.

- *Double Indent* (Ctrl+Shift+F7)
  To move the entire body of a paragraph in from both the left and the right margins, choose Format, Paragraph, Double Indent.

- *Hanging Indent* (Ctrl+F7)
  Choosing Format, Paragraph, Hanging Indent is useful if you need to create a numbered list. ("Hanging Indent" means that in a numbered list, turnovers align with the first word above, not with the number.)

- *Back Tab*
  Choosing Format, Paragraph, Back Tab causes the first line of a paragraph to extend into the left margin, for a distance of one tab stop.

In the following sections, you will use indenting commands to edit WPTEMP to look like Figure 2.6.

1. The WPTEMP document should be displaying on the screen.

2. Position the cursor to the left of the "T" of "The ideal room temperature."

3. PRESS: Enter

4. To indent the text along both margins 1 inch:
   CHOOSE: Format, Paragraph, Double Indent
   CHOOSE (again): Format, Paragraph, Double Indent
   Note: Each time you choose the DOUBLE INDENT command, the rest of the paragraph indents ½ inch.

Figure 2.6

The WPTEMP document after using indent commands

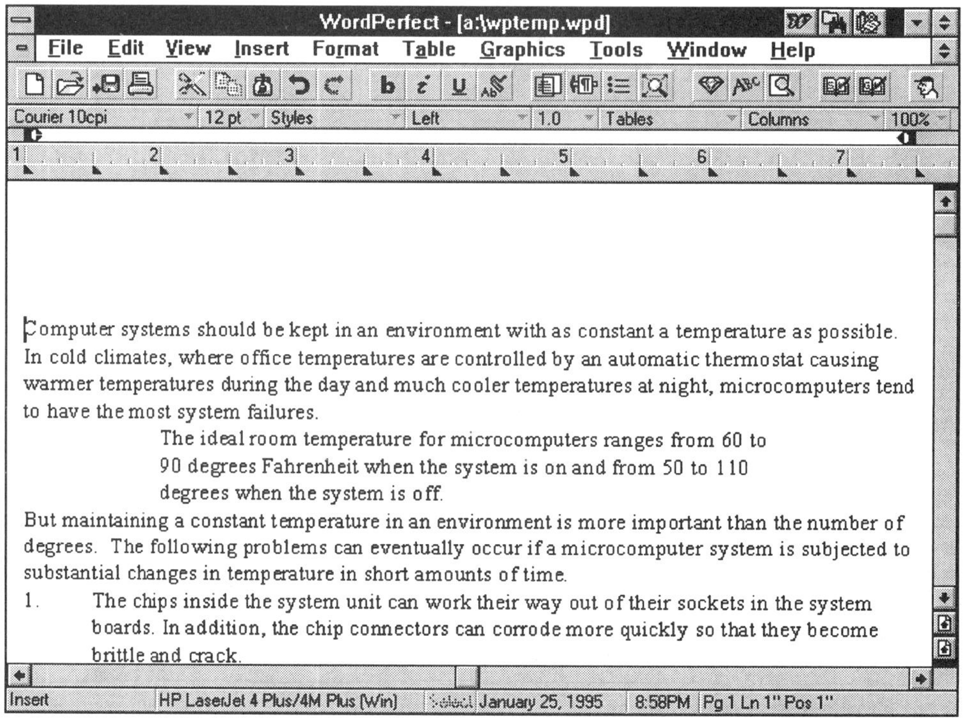

5. At this point, the rest of the paragraph is indented along both margins. To insert an HRt (hard return) code, or **Enter** code, after the first indented sentence, position the cursor before the "B" of "But maintaining."

6. PRESS: **Enter**
   The last sentence should now conform to the default margin settings (1-inch left, 1-inch right).

To add the new text and numbered points:

1. Position the cursor a few spaces to the right of the last sentence in this document.
   TYPE: `The following problems can eventually occur if a microcomputer system is subjected to`

`substantial changes in temperature in short amounts of time:`
PRESS: Enter

2. To type the first numbered point:
CHOOSE: Format, Paragraph, Hanging Indent
TYPE: `1.`
PRESS: Tab
TYPE: `The chips inside the system unit can work their way out of their sockets in the system boards. In addition, the chip connectors can corrode more quickly so that they become brittle and crack.`
PRESS: Enter

3. Before typing the second numbered point, use the keyboard shortcut for creating a hanging indent.
PRESS: Ctrl+F7
TYPE: `2.`
PRESS: Tab
TYPE: `Hard disks suffer from dramatic changes in temperature, which can cause read/write problems. If a new hard disk drive has been shipped in a cold environment, manufacturers usually recommend that users wait for a few hours to a day before operating the hard disk.`
PRESS: Enter

4. To finish the document:
TYPE: `These problems are caused by the expansion and contraction that naturally occur when materials are heated and then cooled. The bottom line is that changes in temperature are stressful for microcomputer systems.`

5. With your cursor at the top of the document, your screen should look similar to Figure 2.6. At this point, close the document and do not save the changes. *Note*: When you close a document, the Ruler bar disappears. You'll have to choose it again to display it when you are working with the next document.

Quick Reference
Indenting

The first line of a paragraph:
PRESS: Tab

Along the left margin:
CHOOSE: Format, Paragraph, Indent, or
PRESS: F7

Along both margins:
CHOOSE: Format, Paragraph, Double Indent, or
PRESS: Ctrl+Shift+F7

For numbered lists:
CHOOSE: Format, Paragraph, Hanging Indent, or
PRESS: Ctrl+F7

Changing Justification

Justification refers to how text aligns with the margins of a document. WordPerfect for Windows provides four different types of justification or alignment for paragraphs: left, right, center, and full. Left justification aligns text at the left margin but provides jagged right edges as a typewriter does. Right justification positions text flush against the right margin but leaves the left side of the text unaligned. Center justification centers the line or each line in a paragraph between the margins. Full justification provides even text alignment at both the left and right margins, like this paragraph, by automatically spacing words on a line. The default justification for WordPerfect is left.

You can apply different justification styles to different paragraphs in your document. To specify justification, use the Justification button located on the Power bar (Left), or choose Format, Justification. The justification for a paragraph can be applied either before or after text is typed. Remember, before you can change the justification of a block of text, you must select it. Otherwise, the entire document is affected downward from where the justification code is inserted.

Perform the following steps to center the title:

1. Open the ETHICS document from the Advantage Diskette that is located in either drive A: or drive B:.

2. SELECT: the title

3. To change the justification of the title:
   CLICK: Justification button (Left)
   SELECT: Center option
   The title should now be centered.
   Note: The Justification button is now displaying "Center" because the currently selected text is centered. If you move the cursor into the paragraph, the Justification button will display an "Left".

Perform the following steps to fully justify the entire document beginning with the first paragraph:

1. PRESS: **Ctrl**+**Home**

2. To change the justification of the rest of the document to Full justification:
   CLICK: Justification button (Left)
   SELECT: Full option
   The rest of the document should now be fully justified.

(Remember that unless you have selected text previously, the document is affected from the cursor position downward.)

3. Keep the ETHICS document open for the discussion of line spacing in the next section.

Quick Reference
Changing Justification

Using the Power bar:
To change the justification of a block of text:
First select the text. Then click the Justification button (Left). Choose the appropriate justification option.

To change the justification of the rest of the document:
First position the cursor where you want the justification code to begin taking effect. Then click the Justification button (Left). Choose the appropriate justification option.

Changing Line Spacing

Another paragraph formatting option allows you to change the line spacing in a document. The standard selections for line spacing—single-spaced, 1½-line-spaced, and double-spaced—can be accessed using the

Line Spacing button (1.0) on the Power bar. You can also specify the exact spacing between lines by choosing the Other option. Using the keyboard, choose Format, Line, Spacing to change line spacing. The default line spacing in WordPerfect is single-spaced.

You can apply different line spacing to different paragraphs in your document. The line spacing code can be inserted either before or after text is typed. Remember, before you can change the line spacing of a block of text, you must select it. Otherwise, the entire document is affected downward from where the line spacing code is inserted.

To practice changing the line spacing of selected text, perform the following steps to change the line spacing of the first paragraph of the ETHICS document from single to double:

1. SELECT: the first paragraph

2. To insert the double-spacing code:
   CLICK: Line Spacing button (1.0)
   SELECT: 2.0 option
   The first paragraph should now be double-spaced.

3. Close the document and do not save the changes.

Quick Reference
Changing the Line Spacing

1. Position the cursor where you want the code to begin taking effect or select the text you want to change.
2. CLICK: Line Spacing button (1.0)
3. SELECT: a spacing option

CREATING BULLETS AND NUMBERED LISTS

WordPerfect offers a utility for creating lists that use a hanging indent with leading **bullets** or numbers. Although round dots are the standard shape for bullets, you can select from a variety of symbols. A numbered list can use roman numerals, letters, or the standard numbering scheme.

The Insert Bullet button () is used for creating bullets and numbered lists. If you select bullets using the toolbar, they will appear as the default round dot, or as previously defined using the Menu bar. To customize how bullets appear, you must choose Insert, Bullets & Numbers. When choosing Insert, Bullets & Numbers, the dialog box in Figure 2.7 appears.

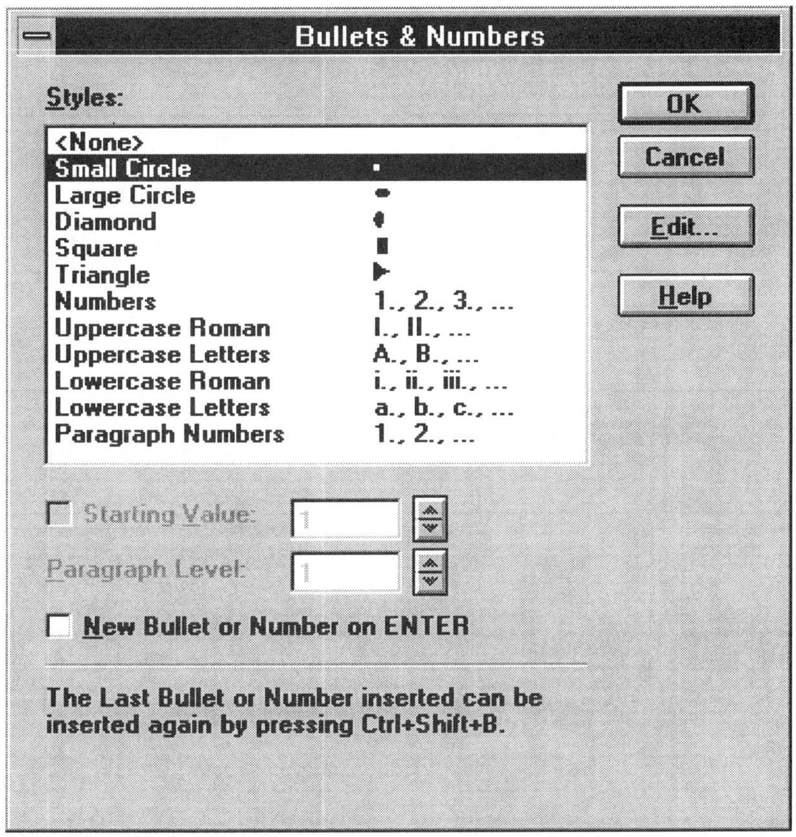

Figure 2.7

Bullets and Numbers dialog box

Perform the following steps to create a new document with bulleted and numbered lists:

1. If the document window isn't empty:
   CHOOSE: File, New
   PRESS: **Enter** *to create a blank document*

2. TYPE: `To Do List`
   PRESS: **Enter** *twice*

3. Enter the following items of text, pressing **Enter** at the end of each line.

```
Pick up dry cleaning
Cash check from work
Go grocery shopping
Send letter to mom
```

4. PRESS: **Enter** *twice*

5. TYPE: Travel Kit
   PRESS: **Enter** *twice*

6. Enter the following lines of text, as before.

```
Toothbrush
Toothpaste
Shampoo
Swim wear
```

7. To create a numbered list out of the To Do List items, first select all four lines of text so they appear in reverse video.

8. CHOOSE: Insert, Bullets and Numbers *from the Menu bar*
   SELECT: Numbers option *in the Styles list box*
   PRESS: **Enter** or CLICK: OK

9. To create a bulleted list out of the Travel Kit items, select the four lines of text so they appear in reverse video.

10. CHOOSE: Insert, Bullets and Numbers *from the Menu bar*
    SELECT: Small Circle option *in the Styles list box*
    PRESS: **Enter** or CLICK: OK

11. To use letters rather than numbers for the To Do List items, select the items again.

12. CHOOSE: Insert, Bullets and Numbers *from the Menu bar*
    SELECT: Lowercase Letters option *in the Styles list box*
    PRESS: **Enter** or CLICK: OK

13. CLICK: *anywhere in the document to remove the highlighting*
    Your document should now look like Figure 2.8.

Figure 2.8

Numbered and bulleted lists

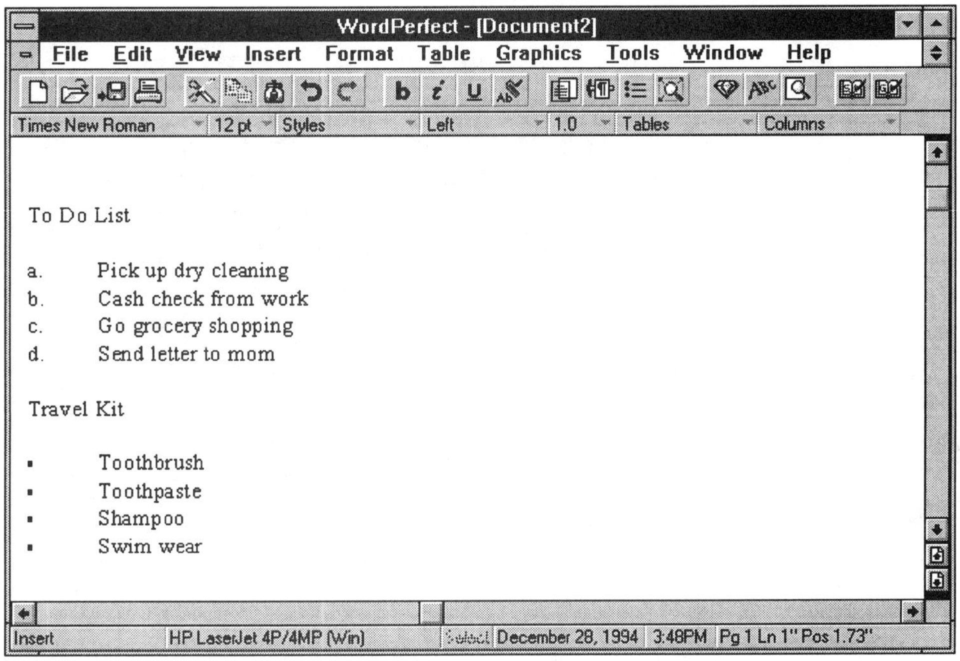

14. To remove the bullets from the Travel Kit list, select the four items under the Travel kit heading.

15. CHOOSE: Insert, Bullets and Numbers *from the Menu bar*
    SELECT: <None> *in the Styles list box*
    PRESS: **Enter** or CLICK: OK

16. Save the document under the name LISTS onto the Advantage Diskette.

17. Close the document.

Quick Reference
Creating Bulleted and Numbered Lists

1. Select the paragraphs or lines for the list.
2. To create a bulleted or numbered list:
   CLICK: Insert Bullet button

   To customize a bulleted or numbered list:
   CHOOSE: Insert, Bullets & Numbers
   SELECT: a style in the Styles list box
   PRESS: **Enter** or CLICK: OK

Changing Tab Settings

Tabs enable you to neatly enter text into columns. For example, rather than using the Space Bar to move the cursor 10 character spaces in from the left margin, you press Tab twice. By default, WordPerfect supplies tabs every ½ inch. Although these settings work well for standard text, some applications, such as numeric tables, require customized tabs. To facilitate data entry, customized tabs are usually set before entering the text. Nevertheless, tab settings are easily inserted, deleted, or modified. There are four different types of tabs available in WordPerfect, as explained in Table 2.7.

Table 2.7

Types of Tabs in WordPerfect

Type	Description
Left-Aligned	Starting at the tab, text extends to the right as you type. By default, WordPerfect's initial tabs are left-aligned.
Center-Aligned	Starting at the tab, text is centered on the tab mark.
Right-Aligned	Starting at the tab, text extends to the left as you type.
Decimal-Aligned	At the tab, the integer portion of a number extends to the left and the decimal portion extends to the right.

You can set tabs for a part of the document by selecting text first and then inserting the tab setting code, or for the rest of the document by positioning the cursor where you want the tab code to begin taking effect and then inserting the tab setting code.

When setting tabs, you can also select a leader for the tab. A **tab leader** is a dotted line that fills the space between text and tab settings. Leaders are commonly used in tables of contents to join the headings with the page numbers.

Tabs are set using the Menu bar or the Tab Set button ( ) in the Toolbar. The procedures for setting tabs are described below:

1. *Setting tabs using the Menu bar*. Choose Format, Line, Tab Set. The dialog box in Figure 2.9 will display. WordPerfect will also display the

Ruler bar. To set a new tab, specify the tab type and position and then select Set. When you're finished selecting tabs, select OK. (*Note*: Users often choose Clear All in the Tab Set dialog box to clear the current tab line before setting new tabs.)

2. *Setting tabs using the Tab Set button* ( ) *on the Toolbar*. Click the Tab Set button on the Format Toolbar and the Tab Set dialog box in Figure 2.9 will display.

3. *Setting tabs using the Ruler.* Choose View, Ruler bar so that the ruler appears at the top of your document. Double-click on one of the default tab markers to bring up the Tab Set dialog box in Figure 2.9. Once your tabs are set, you can drag the tab settings on the ruler to a new location using the mouse.

Figure 2.9

The Tab Set dialog box

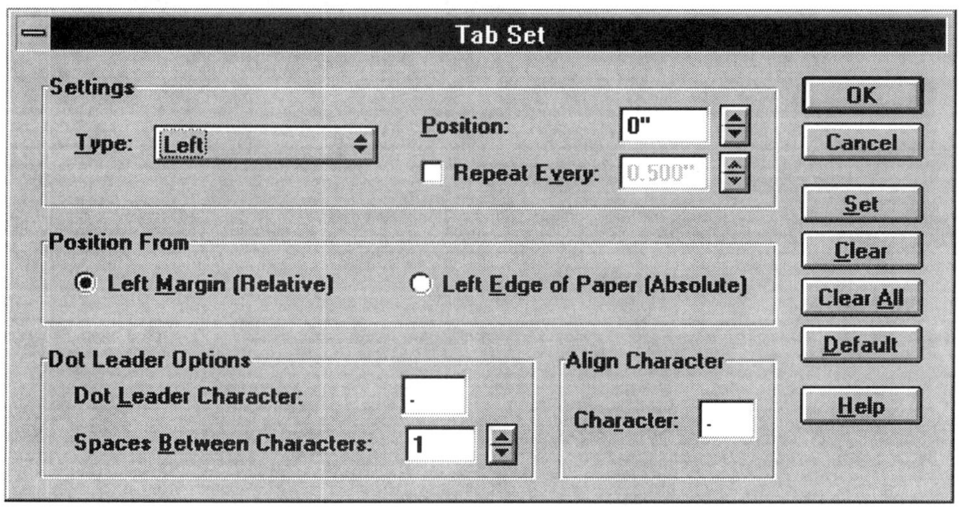

One thing to keep in mind is that WordPerfect measures tabs from the left margin position; that is, by default, the Left Margin button is chosen in the Position From box in the Tab Set dialog box. Therefore, if you set a tab in position 1.5", the tab will be in position 2.5" on the printed page. Similarly, a tab set in position 2" will be in position 3" on the printed page. If you want WordPerfect to position tabs in reference to the edge of the paper, click Left Edge of Paper in the Position From box in the Tab Set dialog box.

In this section, you will create a small document named SALES (pictured in Figure 2.10) to practice changing the tab settings in a document. You will create a Left Tab and two Decimal Tabs that will be used for lining up text and numbers relating to the income and expenses of a sporting goods store named Sporting Life. You will perform the following activities:

- Type in a paragraph using double-spacing.
- Use the Tab Set dialog box to delete the current tab settings.
- Type in the table information.

Figure 2.10
SALES

It is my pleasure to announce to Sporting Life's sales staff that sales have increased steadily for the past six months. As you know, Sporting Life is known for carrying quality sporting items at reasonable prices. But without you, Sporting Life would be "just another sports store." Keep up the good work!

	INCOME	EXPENSES
January	18,900.75	13,534.67
February	22,050.00	15,356.48
March	17,354.45	11,225.32
April	18,239.00	15,006.95
May	26,884.69	19,322.55
June	28,677.41	21,632.10

Perform the following steps to begin a new document and change the line spacing:

1. Your screen should look as it does when you first load WordPerfect. If not, to clear the screen so you can begin working on a new document:
   CHOOSE: File, New

2. To change the line spacing to double:
   CLICK: Line Spacing button (1.0)
   SELECT: 2.0 option
   The text you type will now appear double-spaced.

3. TYPE: `It is my pleasure to announce to Sporting Life's sales staff that sales have increased steadily for the past six months. As you know, Sporting Life is known for carrying quality sporting items at reasonable prices. But`

`without you, Sporting Life would be "just another sports store." Keep up the good work!`
PRESS: **Enter**

Perform the following steps to change the tab settings in the document:

1. The cursor should now be positioned below the paragraph you just typed (on the next line).

2. In this step you will type the headings for the table using the current tab settings:
   PRESS: **Tab** *six times*
   TYPE: `INCOME`
   PRESS: **Tab** *twice*
   TYPE: `EXPENSES`
   PRESS: **Enter** *once*
   The cursor is now in the correct location (one line below the INCOME and EXPENSES headings) for changing the tabs.

3. Before setting up new tabs, you will first delete the current tab settings. Perform the following steps:
   CHOOSE: Format, Line, Tab Set
   To clear the current tab line:
   CLICK: Clear All
   Note that the tab indicators have disappeared from the tab line. The Tab Set dialog box is still displaying.

4. To set a Left Tab that is 1½ inches from the left margin:
   SELECT: the number *located in the Position text box*
   TYPE: `1.5`
   CLICK: Set button

5. To set a Decimal Tab that is 3 inches from the left margin:
   CLICK: Type list box and hold down the left mouse button, while dragging down to select the Decimal option
   SELECT: the number *located in the Position text box*
   TYPE: `3`
   CLICK: Set button

6. To set a Decimal Tab that is 4½ inches from the left margin:
   SELECT: the number *located in the Position text box*
   TYPE: `4.5`
   CLICK: Set button
   CLICK: OK *to return to the document*

7. To enter January's INCOME and EXPENSES figures:
   PRESS: Tab
   TYPE: `January`
   PRESS: Tab
   TYPE: `18,900.75`
   PRESS: Tab
   TYPE: `13,534.67`
   PRESS: Enter

8. Enter the following information to finish the income and expense statement:

	INCOME	EXPENSES
February	22,050.00	15,356.48
March	17,354.45	11,225.32
April	18,239.00	15,006.95
May	26,884.69	19,322.55
June	28,677.41	21,632.10

9. Save the document as SALES onto the Advantage Diskette. Your document should now appear similar to Figure 2.10.

Quick Reference
Tab Settings

1. Clearing tabs:
   CHOOSE: Format, Line, Tab Set
   CHOOSE: Clear All
2. SELECT: *a tab type*
3. SELECT: *a tab position*
4. CLICK: Set
5. Continue setting tabs. When finished:
   CLICK: OK

FORCING A PAGE BREAK

WordPerfect automatically repaginates a document as you insert and delete text. A dotted line appears on the screen wherever WordPerfect inserts a floating page break. ("Floating" means that the position changes as text is added or deleted.) Sometimes the floating page break splits an important paragraph or a table of figures. Rather than leaving the text divided across pages, you can force a hard page break before the text to start a new page. To insert a hard, or forced, page break, press Ctrl+Enter.

In the following steps, you force a page break so that the table created in the SALES document appears on a new page.

1. Position the cursor at the beginning of the line containing the headings INCOME and EXPENSES. Make sure that the cursor is in the first column, next to the left margin.

2. PRESS: Ctrl+Enter
   A solid line appears above the headings line. Note that the cursor is now on page 2. If you were to print the SALES document right now, the table would print out at the top of page 2.

3. To see the code you just inserted in the document, use the REVEAL CODES command:
   CHOOSE: View, Reveal Codes
   You should see the hard page code (HPg) against the left margin. *Note*: When WordPerfect begins a new page on its own, a "soft page" (SPg) code is inserted in your document.

4. To delete the Hard Page code (Hpg), position the cursor to the right of or below the code and press BackSpace or highlight the code and press Delete. The table should again be on page 1.

Note: You can delete the Hard Page code (HPg) without revealing codes by first positioning the cursor at the end of the line that precedes the solid page break line and then pressing Delete.

5. To leave the Reveal Codes screen and return to your document:
   CHOOSE: View, Reveal Codes

Quick Reference
Inserting a Forced Page Break

1. Position the cursor at the beginning of the line that you want moved to the top of a new page.
2. PRESS: Ctrl+Enter
3. To remove the page break, reveal the document codes (View, Reveal Codes) and then position the cursor either on top of the Hard Page code (Hpg) and press Delete or to the right of the code and press BackSpace.

PRINTING A DOCUMENT

Now that you have learned how to create and format documents, this section explains how to send them to the printer. (Session 4 covers specific information regarding page layout and printer setup.) To send a document to the printer, choose File, Print, or click the Print button on the toolbar (🖶). The resulting Print dialog box, as displayed in Figure 2.11, contains options for specifying the number of copies to print and limiting the print selection area. Make the desired selections and then press Enter or choose Print.

Figure 2.11

Print dialog box

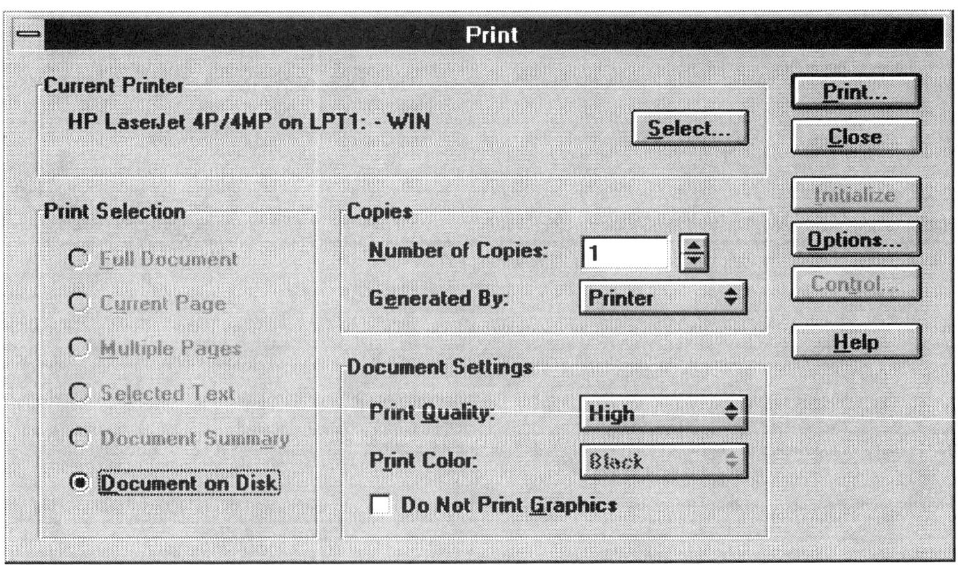

Perform the following steps to print the SALES document.

1. Before printing the SALES document, move to the beginning of the document:
   PRESS: Ctrl+Home

2. CHOOSE: File, Print

3. Accept the default selections to print one copy of the entire document:
   PRESS: Enter *or* CHOOSE: Print

There are several other considerations for printing documents that are covered in Session 4 of this guide.

4. Close the document and, if prompted, do not save the changes.

Quick Reference
Printing a Document

1. CHOOSE: File, Print from the menu, or
2. CLICK: Print button on the Toolbar ()
2. Press Enter or choose Print.

SUMMARY

This section introduced several methods for moving around a document and selecting text. As with most Windows programs, text selection is an extremely important factor for working effectively in WordPerfect. WordPerfect is based upon a "Select" and then "Do" approach to formatting and editing. For example, to format a sentence, you must first select the sentence and then issue the character and paragraph formatting commands.

Character and paragraph formatting commands were discussed in this session. Besides applying boldface, italic, and underlines to text, character formatting involves changing the typeface and point size (font). Paragraph formatting commands enable you to customize paragraphs in your text without affecting the entire document. This section explored indenting paragraphs, aligning or justifying text, using bullets and numbers, setting tabs, and forcing page breaks. The session ended with an opportunity to print a document.

Command Summary

The table on the following page provides a summary of the commands introduced in this session.

Table 2.8

Command Summary	*COMMAND*	*TOOLBAR OR POWER BAR BUTTON*	*TASK*
CHARACTER FORMATTING	Format, Font, Bold	b	Boldface
	Format, Font, Italic	i	Italic
	Format, Font, Underline	u	Single underline
	Format, Font, Double Underline		Double underline
	Format, Font, Font Face	Times New Roman	Typeface selection
	Format, Font, Font Size	12 pt	Point size selection
PARAGRAPH FORMATTING	Format, Line, Tab Set		Specify tab positions and leaders
	Format, Paragraph, Indent		Left indent
	Format, Paragraph, Double Indent		Left and right indent
	Format, Paragraph, Hanging Indent		Hanging indent
	Format, Paragraph, Back Tab		Extend first line of paragraph into left margin of one tab stop.
	Format, Justification	Left	Change the justification to Left, Right, Center, or Full
	Format, Line, Spacing	1.0	Change the line spacing of the document

File, Print, Print		Print the document using WordPerfect's default assumptions

KEY TERMS

bullets Dots, squares, or other figures used to denote new items in an unnumbered list.

default settings Assumptions made by WordPerfect for Windows, if no other specific selections are made.

font All the symbols and characters of a particular typeface in a specific point size. Windows programs use the terms *font* and *typeface* interchangeably.

tab leader The symbols, lines, dots, or dashes that fill the gap between text and tab settings.

typeface The style or design of printed characters.

EXERCISES

SHORT ANSWER

1. You're formatting a document that contains three paragraphs. What procedure should you use to change the line spacing for the second paragraph to double-spacing?
2. What is the procedure for applying bold, italic, and underlines to text?
3. What is the procedure for displaying the Ruler bar?
4. What different types of justification are available?
5. What is a hanging indent?
6. What is the main difference between indenting text and changing the margins?
7. Provide an example of when you would use a dot leader.
8. How would you set line spacing to 2.5 lines?
9. How do you force a hard page break?
10. What is the difference between a hard page break and a floating, or soft, page break?

HANDS-ON

(*Note*: In the following exercises, save your documents onto and retrieve files from the Advantage Diskette.)

1. Create the memo appearing in Figure 2.12. Make sure to include the current date in the DATE: area and your name in the FROM: area of the memo.

Figure 2.12

MEMO document

MEMORANDUM

DATE: *current date*

TO: Kathy Jordan
Administrative Support Manager

FROM: *your name*
V.P., Marketing

SUBJECT: Appearance of Documents

It has come to my attention that our clients are finding our proposals difficult to read. When queried further, they both mentioned (as personal preference dictates) that the sentences seemed to have large gaps between the words. (Similar to this paragraph.)

After speaking with several people in our Word Processing department, I understand that we have been using full justification for paragraphs. As these two clients are our lifeblood, please prepare a letter to the staff stating that the use of full justification in documents is no longer acceptable. All documents are to be typed using left justification only.

Please send me a draft of the letter by next Monday.

Thanks, Kathy — Enjoy your weekend!

a. Make sure that your memo has the following formatting features:
   - center the title "MEMORANDUM"
   - use tabs to right-align the memo headings for DATE:, TO:, FROM:, and SUBJECT:.
   - fully justify the first paragraph
   - left justify the second paragraph
   - right justify the last line

b. Make the title and the memo headings (DATE:, TO:, FROM:, and SUBJECT:) bold.
c. Italicize the word "justification" throughout the memo.
d. Underline "Monday" in the third paragraph.
e. Save the document as MEMO onto the Advantage Diskette.

2. This exercise uses tabs for aligning a table of numbers.
   a. Open a new document.
   b. Specify decimal tab settings of 2", 3.5", and 5.0".
   c. Enter the following information into the document.

	January	February	March
East	50,000	65,000	75,000
West	125,000	105,000	100,500
Central	55,000	50,000	75,000

   d. PRESS: **Enter** *three times*
   e. TYPE: `These are the forecasted commissions for the first part of 1995. Please add a discussion of these figures to the Sales Planning agenda next week.`
   f. Save the document as FORECAST onto the Advantage Diskette.

3. The objective of this exercise is to practice using tabs, leaders, and character formatting commands.
   a. Open a new document.
   b. Create the document appearing in Figure 2.13.
   c. Make the first two lines of the agenda, including the title, date, and time, bold.
   d. Specify a larger font for the title line of the Agenda.
   e. Select a different font for the main agenda items.
   f. Make the three main agenda items bold.
   g. Underline the word "faithful" in the closing of the document.
   h. Save the document as AGENDA onto the Advantage Diskette.

Figure 2.13

AGENDA document

```
                 SALES PLANNING AGENDA

DATE: April 4th, 1995                    TIME: 9am-4pm

Who Is Our Customer?
   Demographic Analysis ................. 9:00-9:45am
   Psychographic Analysis .............. 9:50-10:30am
   Lifestyles and AIO Study ............ 10:45-12noon

What Are We Selling?
   Research and Development ............. 1:00-2:00pm
   Product Packaging .................... 2:05-2:45pm
   Pricing Structures ................... 3:00-3:30pm

Incentives and Commissions .............. 3:35-4:00pm


Please be prepared to give a ten-minute impromptu
presentation on the status of your department.
Specifically, mention the following issues:

-  Employee Productivity
-  Employee Satisfaction
-  Resource Management
-  Future Requirements


                      Your faithful V.P. of Marketing,

                                             your name
```

4. Describe a course you want to take in a document that includes the following:
   a. Tab change
   b. Paragraph indents
   c. Centered title
   d. Your name and the current date
   e. Boldfacing
   f. Underlining
   g. Double-spacing in a portion of the document
   h. Save the document as COURSE.

5. Pretend it is now five years in the future. Use WordPerfect for Windows to create a resume that includes the following information about you: current career objectives, work experience, educational experience, special interests, volunteer activities, and so forth. You may want to organize the resume chronologically beginning with your most recent work experience. You will probably want to perform the following types of tasks:
   a. Center and boldface your name, address, and phone number at the top of the document.
   b. Capitalize and boldface any titles that appear in the resume (for example, the titles for OBJECTIVE, EDUCATION, WORK EXPERIENCE).
   c. Indent any descriptions you include (for example, the description of a job you held in the summer of 1992).
   d. Use underlining and boldfacing for emphasis.
   e. Save this document onto the Advantage Diskette as RESUME.
   f. Print RESUME.

SESSION 3

WORDPERFECT 6.1 FOR WINDOWS: EDITING AND PROOFING TOOLS

The greatest advantage of a word processing program is the ability to modify existing documents. With minimal effort, you can move or copy information and formatting features within a document or among documents. Furthermore, most word processing programs incorporate proofing tools for checking a document's spelling and looking up synonyms for words. These tools, coupled with the editing and formatting features, help you produce high-quality documents.

PREVIEW

When you have completed this session, you will be able to:

Work with several documents at the same time

•

Move text within a document or among documents

•

Copy text within a document or among documents

•

Copy fonts, attributes and paragraph styles

•

Search for and replace text, word forms and codes

•

Add drop caps to a document

•

Perform a spelling check of a document

•

Correct spelling errors while typing

•

Use the thesaurus to find the "perfect" word

SESSION OUTLINE

WHY IS THIS SESSION IMPORTANT?

This session introduces the editing and proofing tools available in WordPerfect for Windows. Besides the standard move and copy commands, WordPerfect provides a Find and Replace utility to search for character- and paragraph-formatting codes as well as text codes and word forms. The significance of this feature rests in WordPerfect's ability to change one formatting enhancement in a document to another with a single command.

WordPerfect's proofing tools include the spell checker, the thesaurus and the QuickCorrect function. Whether you require assistance with spelling or just finding the right word, these tools are invaluable. At the completion of this section, you will have the editing, formatting, and proofing skills to develop high-quality, professional documents.

Before proceeding, make sure the following are true:

1. You have loaded WordPerfect 6.1 for Windows.
2. You have an empty document displayed.
3. Your Advantage Diskette is inserted into drive A: or drive B:. You will save your work onto the diskette and retrieve files that have been created for you. (*Note*: The Advantage Diskette can be duplicated by copying all of the files from your instructor's Master Advantage Diskette.)

WORKING WITH MULTIPLE DOCUMENTS

WordPerfect for Windows allows you to display and work with nine Document windows at once. This feature enables you to easily move and copy information between documents. Furthermore, you can open different window views of a single document to facilitate editing. Each opened document or document view appears in its own Document window. Documents can be viewed vertically or horizontally. These windows can be sized, moved, and arranged anywhere in the Document area.

To practice working with several documents, perform the following steps.

1. Make sure that the Advantage Diskette is inserted into drive A: or drive B:.

2. Close any open document windows that appear in the Document area:
CHOOSE: File, Close

3. Open the document named MANAGER1 from the Advantage Diskette. *Note*: If necessary, refer to Session 1 to review opening a file.

4. Open the document named MANAGER2 from the Advantage Diskette.

5. When the second document is opened, the MANAGER1 document disappears. Actually, the MANAGER2 document is temporarily covering the MANAGER1 document—they are both in memory. To display the MANAGER1 document:
CHOOSE: Window, 1 (MANAGER1)

   Notice that the names of the open documents appear at the bottom of the Window pull-down menu. To move between open documents, simply select the desired document from the pull-down menu.

6. Move back to the MANAGER2 document:
CHOOSE: Window, 2 (MANAGER2)

7. Although this method allows you to switch between documents easily, sometimes it is desirable to compare documents. WordPerfect allows you to view documents either horizontally or vertically. Vertical view allows documents to be viewed side-by-side. Horizontal view positions documents above and below each other.
CHOOSE: Window, Tile Horizontal
Your screen should now appear similar to Figure 3.1.

8. The document window with the scroll bar and highlighted Title bar (MANAGER1) is the active window. As discussed in Session 1, editing and formatting commands affect only the active window. To move between the windows displayed in the document area, use the Window pull-down menu option or a mouse:
CLICK: *anywhere in the MANAGER2 document window*
The MANAGER2 Title bar changes to reflect that it is now the active window.

9. CLICK: *anywhere in the MANAGER1 document window*
   The MANAGER1 Title bar changes to reflect that it is now active.

Figure 3.1

Displaying two documents on the screen in their own Document windows (Window, Tile)

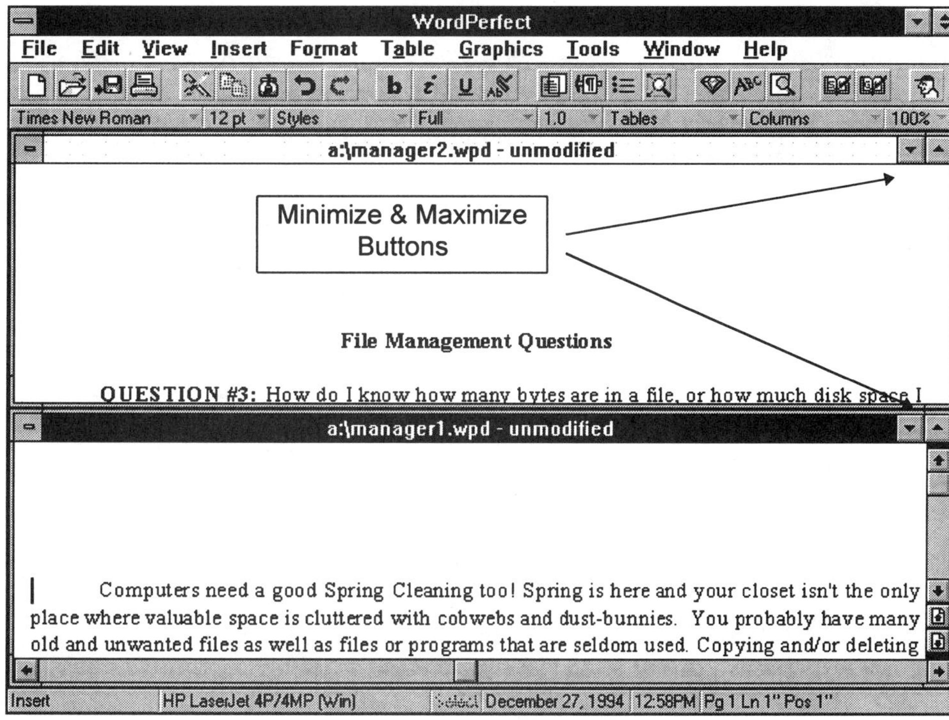

10. Note that each document window has its own Control menu in the upper left-hand corner and a Maximize icon (▲) in the upper right-hand corner. To maximize the MANAGER2 window to fill the entire Document area:
    CLICK: *Maximize icon (▲) of the MANAGER2 document window*
    The MANAGER2 window should be filling the entire Document area.

11. To again arrange the document windows to view both documents at the same time:
    CHOOSE: Window, Tile Vertical *so the documents aren't overlapping*
    Notice that the documents are now positioned side by side.

12. SELECT: *MANAGER1 document window*

13. CHOOSE: File, Close
    The MANAGER1 document is closed and the MANAGER2 document remains as the only open window in the document area.

14. The MANAGER2 window is now current.
    CHOOSE: File, Close *and do not save any changes*

Quick Reference
Working with Several Documents

- CHOOSE: Window, *document name* to display an open document
- CHOOSE: Window, Tile Vertical or Window, Tile Horizontal to display more than one window on the screen at the same time

COPYING AND MOVING INFORMATION

There are several different methods for copying and moving text in a document. As with most Windows applications, WordPerfect uses the **Clipboard**, a Windows utility program, to copy or move information. Once text is placed on the Clipboard, it can be inserted or pasted into multiple WordPerfect documents or Windows applications. In addition, WordPerfect offers **QuickFormat,** which enables you to copy formatting styles throughout your document. One of WordPerfect's most popular features is the **drag and drop** method for copying and moving text within or between documents. This method uses the mouse to simply drag a selected area of text to a desired location, without using the Clipboard. This section provides examples for the three types of editing procedures.

USING THE CLIPBOARD

The Clipboard is used to copy or move information within a document, among documents, or among applications. WordPerfect uses the Edit, Copy option to copy text to the Clipboard and the Edit, Cut option to move text to the Clipboard. Once the selected text is placed on the Clipboard, the Edit, Paste option inserts the text in the desired location. Each of these menu commands has a shortcut key for keyboard users and a Toolbar button for mouse users. A summary of these keyboard and mouse shortcuts appears in Table 3.1.

Table 3.1

Using the Clipboard to Copy and Move Information

COMMAND	SHORTCUTS
Edit, Copy	Ctrl+c, or click button
Edit, Cut	Ctrl+x, or click button
Edit, Paste	Ctrl+v, or click button
Paste Simple	Shift+Ctrl+v

Perform the following steps to practice copying and moving information using the Clipboard.

1. Open the document MANAGER1. Be sure you are at the top of the document:
   PRESS: Ctrl+Home

2. Insert two lines at the top of the document:
   PRESS: Enter *twice*

3. To copy the phrase "Spring Cleaning" from the first sentence to the top of the document, first highlight the text:
   SELECT: "Spring Cleaning"

4. CLICK: Copy button ( )
   The text is copied to the Clipboard in the computer's memory.

5. PRESS: ↑ *three times*

6. CLICK: Paste button ( )
   The text is inserted from the Clipboard and now appears as title.

7. Perform the following steps to format the title.
   SELECT: "Spring Cleaning" *in the title*
   To center the title:
   CLICK: Justification button (Left)
   SELECT: Center option
   Your title should now be centered.

8. The title "Spring Cleaning" should still be highlighted. To change the case of the letters from uppercase/lowercase to all uppercase:
   CHOOSE: Edit, Convert Case, Uppercase

9. The title "Spring Cleaning" should still be highlighted. To make the title appear bold:
   CLICK: Bold button (**b**)

10. To move the second paragraph to the end of the document, first select the paragraph to move:
    SELECT: *the second paragraph*

11. CLICK: Cut button ( )
    The text is moved from the document to the Clipboard.

12. PRESS: Ctrl+End *to move to the end of your document*
    CLICK: Paste button ( )
    The text is inserted at the cursor position.

13. To move the paragraph back, first select the paragraph.
    SELECT: *the paragraph you moved to the bottom of the document*

14. CLICK: Cut button ( )
    The text is removed from the document.

15. Move the cursor to the position beneath the first paragraph where the second paragraph should be inserted.

16. CLICK: Paste button ( )
    The contents of the Clipboard are inserted into the document at the cursor location.

17. When information is placed on the Clipboard, it can be inserted or pasted multiple times. To illustrate, move to the end of the document and click the Paste button ( ):
    PRESS: Ctrl+End
    CLICK: Paste button ( )
    The contents of the Clipboard have been pasted again into the document.

18. To undo the last paste operation:
    CHOOSE: Edit, Undo

WordPerfect also features a **Paste Simple** tool which makes cut or copied text look exactly like the existing text at the insertion point. Using this tool, you can copy or cut text of varying font styles, sizes and attributes and it will be pasted into your document as the default font, color, and size.

Perform the following steps to practice copying and moving information using the Paste Simple tool.

1. Close any open document windows that appear in the Document area. Do not save any changes. Make sure the Advantage Diskette is in Drive A: or Drive B:.

2. Open the document named SIMPLE from the Advantage Diskette.

3. To highlight the first sentence of the document and copy it to the windows Clipboard:
   SELECT: *the first sentence*
   (Hint: Position the cursor before the "A" in the word "Acronyms". Click the left mouse button *three times* to select the sentence.)
   CLICK: Copy button ( )

4. Paste the selected text into the second paragraph, between the first and second sentences, so that it matches the second paragraph formatting. Position the cursor before the letter "I" in "Initials".
   PRESS: Shift+Ctrl+v
   The contents of the Clipboard have been pasted into the second paragraph and match the existing text format of the second paragraph.

The preceding steps introduced you to copying and moving text using the Clipboard. You can apply these commands to copying and moving text to different documents. To copy or move information to another document, use the COPY or CUT commands on the appropriate text, select the other document from the Window pull-down menu, position the mouse pointer in the new document, and then issue the PASTE command.

Note: The Edit, Paste Special command enables you to paste data and objects into your document that were created in other Windows applications. The Edit, Append command allows you to attach selected text or graphics to the end of the current contents of the Clipboard.

Quick Reference
Copying and Moving Using the Clipboard

- To copy information to the Clipboard, choose Edit, Copy, press Ctrl+c, or click the Copy button ()
- To move information to the Clipboard, choose Edit, Cut, press Ctrl+x, or click the Cut button ()
- To insert information into a document, choose Edit, Paste, press Ctrl+v, or click the Paste button ()
- To insert information into a document so that it looks like the existing text at the insertion point, paste the text by pressing Shift+Ctrl+v

QUICKFORMAT

In addition to copying text, WordPerfect offers a utility called **QuickFormat** which enables you to copy fonts, attributes, and paragraph styles from one area of text to another. With QuickFormat, when the text style is changed in one place, the same style is updated automatically in the rest of the document. QuickFormat has two copy choices: Copy characters, which copies only the font and attributes of the current text, or copy headings which additionally copies paragraph formatting such as tabs, indents, centering and style.

Perform the following steps to practice using the QuickFormat function:

1. The document SIMPLE should still be open. If not, retrieve the file SIMPLE from the Advantage Diskette.

2. Copy the formatting features of paragraph two to paragraph one. Position the mouse pointer in front of the "F" in the word "For" in the second paragraph.

3. CLICK: QuickFormat button ()
   The dialog box in Figure 3.2 appears on your screen.

Figure 3.2

QuickFormat dialog box

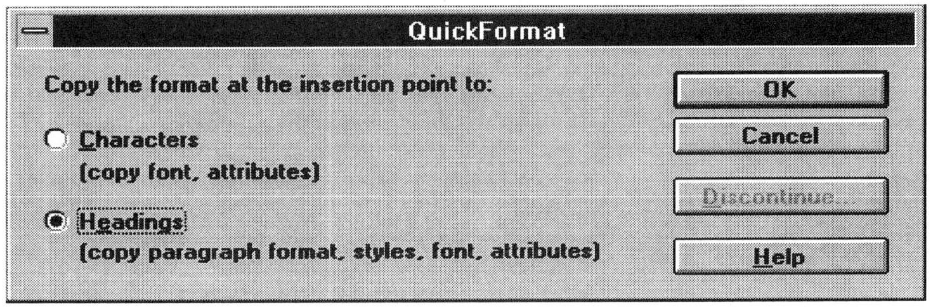

CHOOSE: Headings
PRESS: Enter or CLICK: OK
The mouse pointer changes to an I-Beam and a paintbrush roller.

3. Select the second paragraph as the format to be copied.
   CLICK: left mouse button *once to highlight the second paragraph*

4. Copy the text formatting features to the first paragraph. Move the I-beam paintbrush roller to the beginning of the first paragraph.
   CLICK: left mouse button *once to highlight the first paragraph*
   Notice that the formatting features of the second paragraph have been copied to the first paragraph.

5. Turn off the QuickFormat.
   CLICK: QuickFormat button ()

6. Close the document and do not save the changes.

Quick Reference
Copying font attributes and paragraph formats

- To copy fonts, attributes, and paragraph styles from one area of text to another:
- CLICK: QuickFormat button ()
- CHOOSE Character *to copy fonts and attributes only*
- CHOOSE Headings *to copy all attributes, including paragraph formatting*
- Select the text to be copied and release the mouse button.
- Select the text to be newly formatted and release the mouse button
- CLICK: QuickFormat button () *to turn off QuickFormat*

USING THE DRAG AND DROP METHOD

The drag and drop method is the easiest way to copy and move information short distances. The Clipboard is not used during a drag and drop operation. You can copy or move text from one location to another in the same document, or between multiple documents that are being viewed simultaneously.

Perform the following steps to practice the drag and drop method.

1. Open the document SIMPLE from the Advantage Diskette.

2. Position the cursor before the letter "A" in "Acronyms."
   CLICK: the left mouse button *four times to select the entire paragraph*

3. Position the mouse pointer over the selected text. Notice that the pointer shape is a left-pointing diagonal arrow, and not an I-beam. To move this paragraph using the drag and drop method:
   CLICK: *left mouse button and hold down*

4. When you drag the mouse pointer, it changes shape to include a phantom insertion point at the end of the diagonal arrow.
   DRAG: *mouse pointer downward to the end of the document after the words "Operating System"*
   RELEASE: left mouse button
   The text is moved in its entirety to the new location.

5. To remove the highlighting from the text:
   CLICK: *anywhere in the document*

As we mentioned earlier, sometimes after moving and copying you may have to insert and delete extra lines. WordPerfect will automatically add or delete spaces as needed at the insertion point so that the moved or copied text merges easily. The drag and drop method can also be used to copy text.

1. Select the words "Graphic User Interfaces" in the third paragraph:
   SELECT: "Graphic User Interfaces"
   The words should be highlighted in reverse video.

2. To copy these words beneath the title area:
   PRESS: **Ctrl** *and hold down*

3. Position the mouse pointer over the highlighted words until it changes to a pointing arrow.
   DRAG: *the mouse pointer upward*
   Notice the mouse pointer now displays a plus sign, indicating the copy mode is activated.

4. Position the mouse pointer beneath the word "Computers" in the title area.

5. Release the left mouse button. The text has been copied to the title area.

6. Perform the following steps to format the highlighted text:
   CHOOSE: Edit, Convert Case, Uppercase
   CLICK: Bold button (**b**)

7. Close the document and do not save the changes.

Quick Reference
Using Drag and Drop

- To move information, first select the text to move. Then position the mouse pointer over the selected text and click and hold down the left mouse button. Drag the selected text to the desired location and then release the left mouse button.
- To copy information, first select the text to copy and then press **Ctrl** and hold down. Now position the mouse pointer over the selected text and click and hold down the left mouse button. Drag the selected text to the desired location and then release the left mouse button.
- To move or copy information between documents, tile the documents either vertically or horizontally and use drag and drop to copy or move information between documents.

SEARCHING FOR AND REPLACING TEXT

Imagine that you just completed a 200-page proposal supporting the importation of llamas as pets in North America. As you are printing the final pages, a colleague points out that you spelled llama with one *l* throughout the document. The spell checker didn't catch the error since both *llama*, the animal, and *lama*, the Tibetan monk, appear in

WordPerfect's dictionary. Therefore, you must use another of WordPerfect's editing features—the Find and Replace utility—to correct this mistake.

The Find and Replace command under the Edit menu allows you to search for and replace text in a document. The keyboard shortcut for the FIND and REPLACE command is F2. Perform the following steps.

1. Make sure that the Advantage Diskette is inserted into drive A: or drive B:.

2. Close any open Document windows that appear in the Document area:
   CHOOSE: File, Close

3. Open the document named REPORT from the Advantage Diskette.

4. To search for the occurrence of a word or phrase in a document:
   CHOOSE: Edit, Find and Replace, *or*
   PRESS: F2
   The Find and Replace Text dialog box appears, as displayed in Figure 3.3.

Figure 3.3

Find and Replace Text dialog box

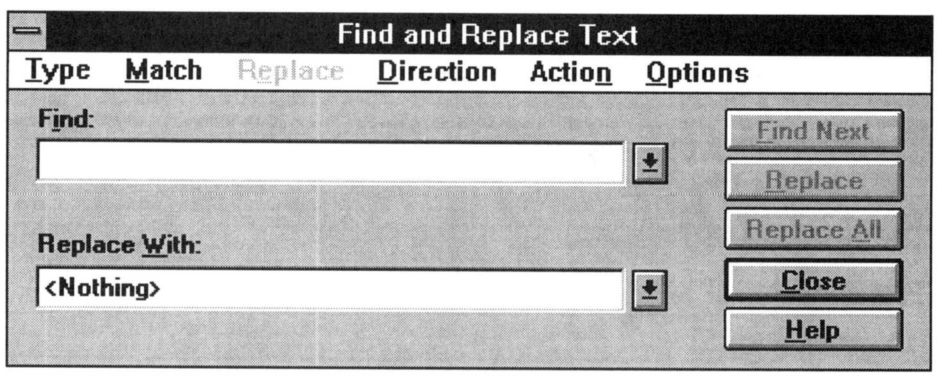

5. With the cursor in the Find text box, enter the text to be found:
   TYPE: `gorilla`
   Do not type text in the Replace With text box. Accept the default, <Nothing>.
   CLICK: Find Next button

6. WordPerfect stops at the first occurrence of the word "gorilla." To continue the search:
   CLICK: Find Next button
   The cursor should be highlighting each occurrence of the word "gorilla."

7. Continue the search by clicking the Find Next button. When "gorilla" is no longer found, WordPerfect will display a message on the screen indicating that the text string you're searching for can't be found.

8. CLICK: OK button *to display the Find Text dialog box*
   CLICK: Close button *to display the document*

Quick Reference
Searching for Text

1. CHOOSE: Edit, Find and Replace *from the menu, or*
   PRESS: F2
2. TYPE: *text to search for* and then click Find Next button
3. After finding an occurrence, choose Find Next button to continue the search.

The next series of steps shows how to replace text and formatting in a document.

1. Start the replace operation at the top of the document:
   PRESS: Ctrl+Home

2. CHOOSE: Edit, Find and Replace

3. Enter the text to replace in the Find text box:
   TYPE: `gorilla`
   PRESS: Tab *once*
   Note: If you completed the last section, "gorilla" is already displaying in the Find text box.

4. Enter the replacement text in the Replace With text box:
   TYPE: `chimpanzee`
   Your screen should appear similar to Figure 3.4.

Figure 3.4

Find and Replace dialog box

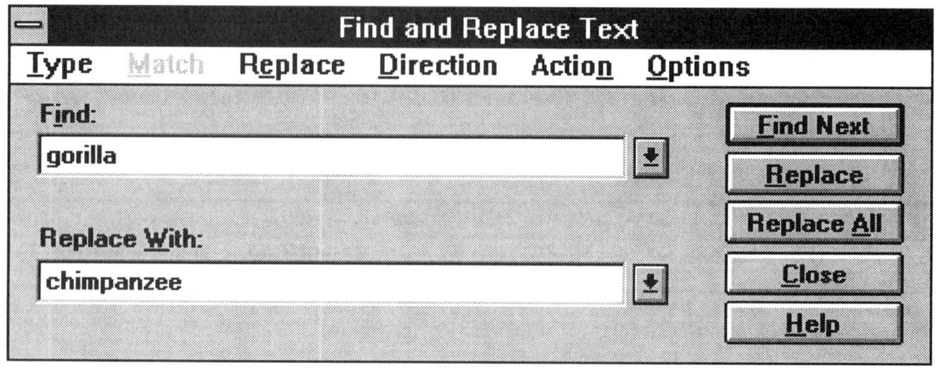

CLICK: Find Next button

5. After the first occurrence of the word "gorilla" appears, you can continue with the search, or replace the text and continue, or cancel the search. To replace the text and continue:
   CLICK: Replace button
   WordPerfect proceeds to the next occurrence of the word.

6. To change all of the occurrences of the word "gorilla" to "chimpanzee":
   CLICK: Replace All button

7. When finished with the search and replace, leave the dialog box:
   CLICK: Close button

8. To return to the beginning of your document:
   PRESS: Ctrl+Home

The Find and Replace utility also enables you to search for specific codes, such as margins, justification, underline and boldface codes. You use the same procedure to find codes as you do to find text.

1. Let's apply boldface to all occurrences of the word "western".
   CHOOSE: Edit, Find and Replace

2. Type the text you're searching for in the Find text box:
   TYPE: `western`
   PRESS: Tab *once*

3. Type the text you're replacing with in the Replace With box. To specify the boldface attribute, you must insert the [Bold On] code before `western` and the [Bold Off] code after `western`:
   TYPE: `western`
   PRESS: **Home** *to move the cursor is to the left of* `western`
   CHOOSE: Replace, Codes *from the "Find and Replace Text" menu that is displaying at the top of the dialog box*
   SELECT: Bold on code *from the Replace Codes box (you will have to drag the scroll bar downward to see the code)*
   CLICK: Insert button
   CLICK: Close button
   PRESS: **End** *to move the cursor is to the right of the word* `western`
   CHOOSE: Replace, Codes *from the "Find and Replace Text" menu that is displaying at the top of the dialog box*
   SELECT: Bold on code *from the Replace Codes box (you will have to drag the scroll bar downward to see the code)*
   CLICK: Insert button
   CLICK: Close button

4. CLICK: Replace All button

5. CLICK: Close button
   Browsing through the document, you will notice that each occurrence of the word western is boldfaced.

6. Close the document and do not save the changes.

Quick Reference
Replacing Text or Codes

1. CHOOSE: Edit, Find and Replace *from the Menu bar, or*
   PRESS: **Ctrl**+**F2**
2. TYPE: *the text you want to replace*
   PRESS: **Tab**
3. TYPE: *replacement text*
   PRESS: **Enter**

(Note: To find (or replace) codes in a document, choose Replace, Codes from the dialog box menu.

4. After finding the first occurrence, select Find, Replace, Replace All, or Close.

DROP CAPS

Drop Caps is a WordPerfect feature that enables you to enlarge the first character, letters, word or words of a paragraph. This editing feature gives a dynamic, desktop-publishing look to your documents. You can either create a drop cap as you begin typing a new paragraph, or you can create a drop cap for an existing paragraph. To create a drop cap as you type, choose Drop Cap from the Format menu and begin typing. To add a drop cap to an existing paragraph or document, position the cursor at the insertion point and choose Drop Cap from the Format menu. Drop caps can be customized by using the **Drop cap palette** to specify a desired type, font, position or size. You can also add borders and fill to further customize the look of your drop caps.

Perform the following steps to add drop caps to your document.

1. Open the document MANAGER1 from the Advantage Diskette.

2. Add a drop cap to the first letter of the first paragraph. Move the cursor to the left of the letter "C" in the word "Computers".

3. CHOOSE: Format, Drop Cap

   Your screen should appear similar to Figure 3.5. Notice how the first letter of the paragraph has changed to a large "C". The paragraph text automatically wraps around the drop cap letter. The drop cap pallette is now visible beneath the Power bar.

Figure 3.5

Drop Caps

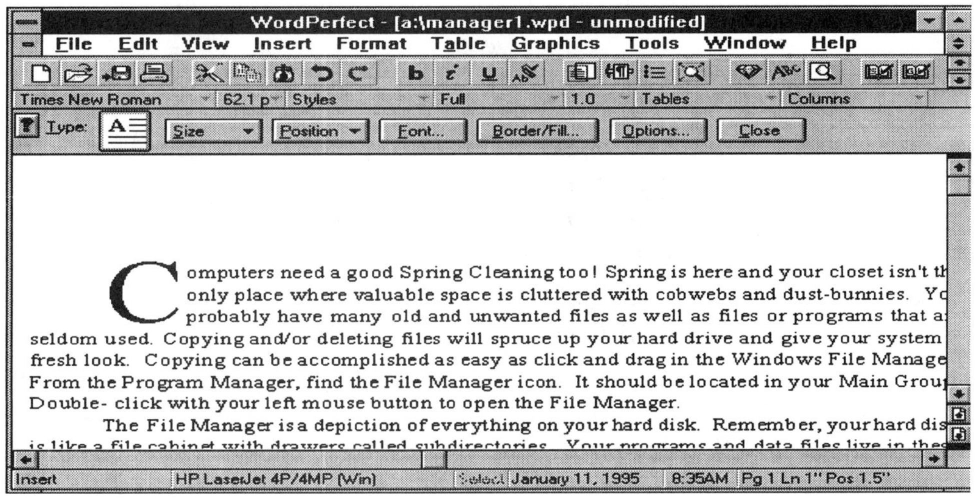

4. To change the type of drop cap:
   CLICK: Type button *on the drop cap palette*
   CLICK: *any of the type options*
   Notice how the drop cap changes in your document. Practice changing the drop cap by choosing various type options. When you are finished, close the drop cap palette.
   CLICK: Close

5. Practice adding a drop cap to the first letter of every paragraph in your document.

6. Close the document and do not save the changes.

Quick Reference
Adding drop caps to your document

1. CHOOSE: Format, Drop Cap
2. CHOOSE: Type *from the drop cap palette to change the look or type of drop cap*
3. After adding and customizing the drop cap:
   CHOOSE: Close *on the drop cap palette*

USING THE SPELL CHECKER

As mentioned at the outset of this session, WordPerfect provides some very useful editing and proofing tools including the spell checker and the thesaurus. This section introduces the **spell checker** and **QuickCorrect** tools for correcting typographical errors and misspellings. You can perform a spelling check on a single word, a selection of text, or the entire document. The SPELL CHECK command is initiated by choosing Tools, Spell Check, pressing Ctrl+F1, or clicking the Spell Check button on the Toolbar (). QuickCorrect corrects errors automatically as you type and is initiated by choosing Tools, QuickCorrect or pressing Shift+Ctrl+F1.

When a spelling check is requested, WordPerfect begins scanning the document downward from the cursor position. Each word is compared to entries made in WordPerfect's main dictionary, which contains 115,000 words. If the word is not found, then WordPerfect attempts to find a match in a supplemental dictionary that you create. Supplemental dictionaries usually contain proper names, technical terms, and abbreviations. The spell checker also scans for duplicate words and gives you the opportunity to delete the repeated word. In the following exercise, you perform a spelling check of a document.

Perform the following steps.

1. Make sure that the Advantage Diskette is inserted into drive A: or drive B:.

2. Open the document named SPELLING.

3. To initiate the SPELL CHECK command:
   CHOOSE: Tools, Spell Check
   The spell checker begins automatically.

   When WordPerfect encounters the first misspelled word, it displays a dialog box (Figure 3.6) and waits for further instructions.

Figure 3.6

Spell Check dialog box

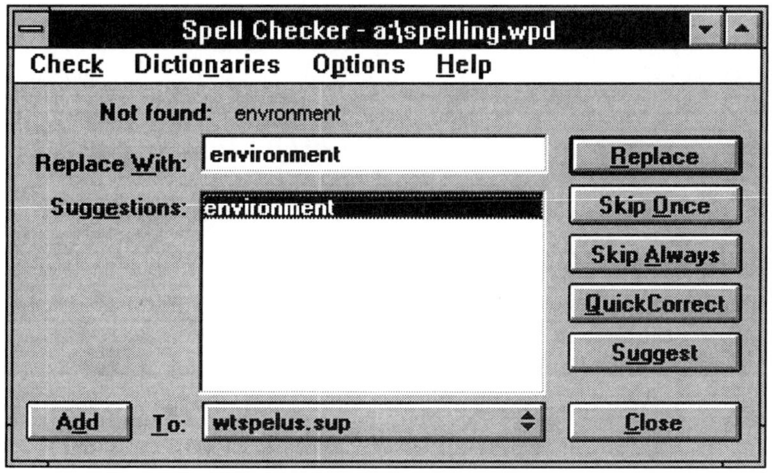

4. You have several options when the spell checker cannot find a word in its dictionary:
   a. If a word is misspelled and the proper version appears in the Suggestions list box, highlight the word in the list box and then select the Replace button.
   b. If the word is misspelled and none of the suggestions is correct, type the proper version into the Replace With text box and select the Replace button.
   c. If the word is spelled correctly and not frequently used, select the Skip Once or Skip Always button to proceed to the next word.
   d. If the word exists in the QuickCorrect utility, choosing this options will automatically correct the word.
   e. If the word is spelled correctly and frequently used, select the Add button to add it to the supplemental dictionary.
   f. If a duplicate word is found, choose Replace.
   g. To end the spelling check, select the Close button.

   To change the misspelled word "westrn" to the suggested spelling of "western":
   CLICK: Replace button

5. Continue the spelling check for the remainder of the document. When it is completed, a message box appears asking if you want to close the spell checker and return to your document:
   CLICK: Yes button

6. Close the document and do not save your changes.

To search a portion, or block, of a document, highlight (select) the block and then activate the spell checker from the Tools menu.

WordPerfect's **QuickCorrect** feature corrects frequently misspelled words as you type. QuickCorrect has its own library of default spelling errors and replacements which can be deleted or edited if you choose. You can also add words to QuickCorrect that may be specific to your own needs.

1. Begin a new document.
   CHOOSE, File, New
   PRESS: Enter *to create a blank document*

2. Add words to the QuickCorrect utility as follows:
   CHOOSE: Tools, QuickCorrect
   TYPE: `alwas` *in the Replace text box*
   TYPE: `always` *in the With text box*
   CHOOSE: Add Entry
   If in the future, if you mistakenly type `alwas` in a document, WordPerfect will automatically insert the word `always` in its place.

3. To disable the QuickCorrect feature, make sure the "Replace Words as You Type" check box has not been checked.

4. CHOOSE: Close

5. Close your document and do not save changes. All changes made to the QuickCorrect utility have been saved for future use with all your documents.

Quick Reference
Using the Spell Check and QuickCorrect

1. CHOOSE: Tools, Spell Check, or
   CLICK: Spell Check button ( )
2. When a misspelled word is located, WordPerfect suggests alternative spellings. Highlight a suggestion and select the Replace button, or skip the word and continue without modification.
3. When a technical term or proper name cannot be found in the main dictionary, add the word to the supplemental dictionary by selecting the Add button.
4. To view and customize the QuickCorrect utility:
   CHOOSE: Tools, QuickCorrect, or
   PRESS: Ctrl+Shift+F1

USING THE THESAURUS

Have you ever found yourself with the "perfect" word at the tip of your tongue—only to have it stay there? Although this situation is not limited to authors and professional writers, most writers know how to find the word using a thesaurus. WordPerfect's **thesaurus** utility provides quick access to synonyms (words with similar meanings) and antonyms (words with opposite meanings) for a given word or phrase. Alternatives to words are arranged as headwords. You can search for alternative meanings in up to three sub-groups. The thesaurus utility is invoked by choosing Tools, Thesaurus from the menu or by pressing Alt+F1.

Perform the following steps to practice accessing the thesaurus.

1. Open the REPORT document on the Advantage Diskette.

2. Select the word "discovered" in the middle of the first sentence in the first paragraph:
   SELECT: `discovered`

3. CHOOSE: Tools, Thesaurus, or
   PRESS: Alt+F1
   The Thesaurus dialog box appears, as displayed in Figure 3.7.

Figure 3.7

Thesaurus dialog box

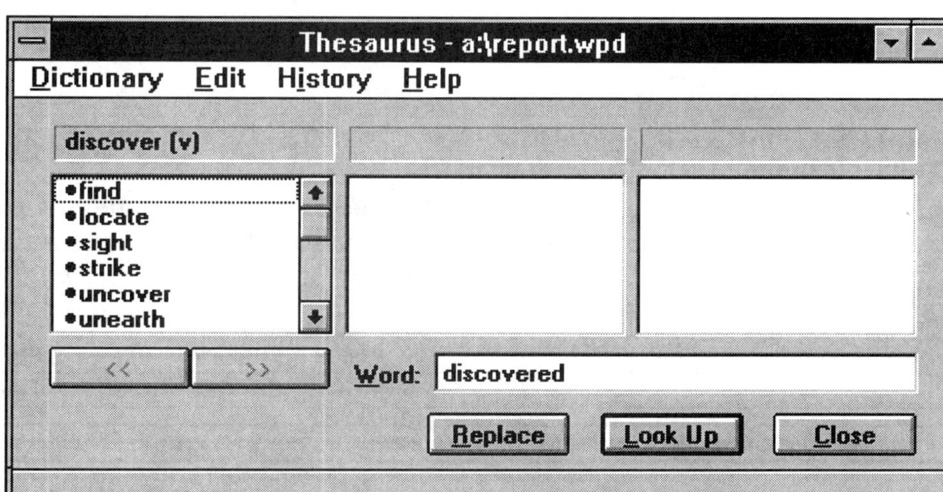

Since a word may have several interpretations, you can select the appropriate meaning from the list box on the left side of the dialog box. This list box displays the synonyms for the word displaying in the Word text box. When you select a synonym, the Word text box is automatically updated with the highlighted synonym. You have four options after selecting a word from the synonyms list box:

a. Select the Replace button to replace the word in the document with the word in the Word text box.
b. Select the Look Up button to display synonyms for the word in the Word text box. *Note*: These words, called headwords, for which the thesaurus provides synonyms, are preceded by a bullet.
c. Double-click on a headword and create a sub-group of additional choices. You can create up to three sub-groups.
d. Type a word into the Word text box and then select the Look Up command button.

4. To change the word "discovered" in the document to "sighted" from the synonyms list box:
   CLICK: "`sight`" *from the synonyms list box*
   CLICK: Replace button
   Notice that WordPerfect automatically adjusted the verb tense of the word to the proper form.

5. Practice using the thesaurus tool in the document REPORT to find synonyms for at least 10 words. Replace each word.

6. Close the document and do not save any changes.

Quick Reference
Using the Thesaurus

1. Select a word to look up in the thesaurus.
2. CHOOSE: Tools, Thesaurus *from the menu, or* press: **Alt**+**F1**
3. Highlight the desired word in the synonyms list box.
4. To display synonyms for the highlighted word, select the Look Up button.
5. To create a sub-group, double-click on a headword.
6. To replace the word in the document with the word in the Word text box, select the Replace button.

SUMMARY

This session introduced the editing and proofing tools available in WordPerfect for Windows. After a discussion on working with multiple windows, the session described the two primary methods for copying and moving information: using the Clipboard and using the drag and drop method. In addition, tools for copying text and paragraph attributes were demonstrated. To conclude the editing tools, we described useful techniques for finding and replacing text and word forms in a document and enhancing documents with drop caps.

The Spell Check and Thesaurus tools were used to proof documents. Spell Check can even add words to a custom dictionary during a spelling check. WordPerfect's thesaurus provides a list of synonyms for words, enabling you to find the right word for expressing yourself. QuickCorrect is used to correct spelling errors as you type and can be customized to your needs.

COMMAND SUMMARY

Table 3.2 provides a list of the commands and procedures covered in this session.

Table 3.2

Command Summary

COMMAND	TASK
Window, *document name*	Select a window to make active
Window, Tile	Display more than one window on the screen at once
Edit, Copy Ctrl+c, or	Copy the selected text to the Clipboard
Format, QuickFormat, or	Copies fonts, attributes, and paragraph styles from one area of text to another.
Edit, Cut Ctrl+x, or	Move the selected text to the Clipboard

Edit, Paste Ctrl+v, or [button]	Insert the contents of the Clipboard at the current cursor location
Ctrl+Shift+v	Paste Simple matches copied text to the existing text formats
Edit, Find and Replace F2	Search for text in a document or search and replace
Format, Drop Cap Ctrl+Shift+c	Add a drop cap to your document
Tools, Spell Check Ctrl+F1 or [button]	Perform a spelling check of a document
Tools, QuickCorrect Ctrl+Shift+F1	Corrects commonly misspelled words as you type
Tools, Thesaurus Alt+F1	Display a list of synonyms for the selected word or phrase

KEY TERMS

Clipboard In Windows, the Clipboard is a program that allows you to copy and move information within an application or among applications.

drag and drop A feature of Windows that allows you to copy and move information by dragging objects or text from one location to another using the mouse.

Drop Cap A feature that allows you to customize paragraph beginnings with styles of drop caps that are pre-defined or tailored.

QuickCorrect A utility that automatically corrects spelling and capitalization errors as you type. This utility can be customized.

QuickFormat A feature that allows you to copy formatting styles throughout your document. Text that has been formatted using the QuickFormat function is automatically updated when the style is changed in another area of the document.

Spell Checker A utility in WordPerfect that helps you to locate and correct misspellings in a document.

Thesaurus A utility in WordPerfect that provides synonyms and antonyms for the selected word or phrase. A synonym is a word that has the same meaning as another word. An antonym has the opposite meaning.

EXERCISES

SHORT ANSWER

1. How can documents be viewed in the document area?
2. How do you move between open documents using the keyboard? Using the mouse?
3. What are the two methods for copying and moving information? How do they differ?
4. Name three uses of the Find and Replace utility.
5. What is the difference between searching for words and word forms?
6. What is the THESAURUS command used for? What options are available in the thesaurus utility?
7. What is the difference between the Spell Check and QuickCorrect utilities?
8. What is the shortcut keyboard method for calling up the thesaurus?
9. What is meant by the phrase *drag and drop*?
10. What does the term "paste simple" mean?

Hands-On

(*Note*: In the following exercises, save your documents onto and retrieve files from the Advantage Diskette.)

1. The objective of this exercise is to practice using the COPY and MOVE commands in WordPerfect.
   a. Create the document appearing in Figure 3.7.
   b. Save the document as ORDERS onto the Advantage Diskette.
   c. Using the Clipboard, move the text after "P.S." (starting at the word "If") above the line "Yours truly." Leave the "P.S." at the bottom of the letter.
   d. Using the Clipboard, move the first sentence in the first paragraph ("Thank you for your order!") after the "P.S." on the last line.
   e. Using the drag and drop method, change the order of the Items Shipped to the following: CPU, HARD DISK, MONITOR, VIDEO CARD, and OPTIONS.
   f. Using the drag and drop method, copy the company name "Alpha Beta Computer Rentals" from the top of the page to below the title "Accounts Representative" in the closing.
   g. Save the document as ORDERS and replace the old version of the file.
   h. Close the document.

Figure 3.8

ORDERS letter

Alpha Beta Computer Rentals
5900 Algonquin Road
Suite 775
Asheville, NC 28804

December 3, 1995

Ms. Lolita Balfour
2910 Freemont Road
Raleigh, NC 27610

Dear Ms. Balfour:

Thank you for your order! I am writing to confirm your order of the following items to be delivered to your premises on December 14th, 1995.

Items Shipped

MONITOR:	TLC MultipleSync 4GH Monitor
OPTIONS:	2400 Baud Internal Modem
HARD DISK:	MaxStore 512 MB Hard Drive
CPU:	Compact 486/33 with 16 MB RAM
VIDEO CARD:	ABC Ultrasonic Graphics Card

Yours truly,

your name
Accounts Representative

P.S. If I can be of any assistance, please call me at 704-555-9987.

2. This exercise gives you practice using the Find and Replace utility. (*Note*: Additional instructions follow in the next page.)
   a. Open the MISDEPT document from the Advantage Diskette (Figure 3.8).

Figure 3.9

MISDEPT memo

DATE: August 14, 1995

TO: Mr. Tyler French
Director of Operations
Management Information Systems Department

FROM: *your name*
your address
your city, state zip code

SUBJECT: OS/5 Version 6.0 Batch Release 2.109

Please be forewarned that the OS/5 Version 6.0 Batch Release 2.109 operating system will not be available for the Management Information Systems Department on January 12, 1995, as previously promised.

Although we understand the requirement for OS/5 Version 6.0 Batch Release 2.109, Research and Development must fully test the product before allowing any department access to the code — and that includes the Management Information Systems Department.

If you require to speak with me, please have Augusta Johansen, V.P. - Management Information Systems Department, contact me at the following address:

your name
your address
your city, state zip code

Thanks for your patience.

b. Find the text "your name" and replace it with your actual name.
c. Find the text "your address" and replace it with your actual address.
d. Find the text "your city, state, and zip code" and replace it with your actual city, state, and zip code information.
e. Using the REPLACE command, change the name of the department from "Management Information Systems Department" to "Office Automation Division."
f. Save the document as MISDEPT and replace the old version.

3. The following exercise involves using the following WordPerfect features: Find and Replace, Speller, and drag and drop.
   a. Close any open documents in the Document window.
   b. Open the ERRORS document from the Advantage Diskette.
   c. Search for the words "`error`", "`pink`", "`peaches`", "`uncle`" and "`doghouse`" and delete them. (*Hint*: Use Find and Replace to find the word and replace with <nothing>. This will delete the unwanted word).
   d. Search for the word "`DOS`" and replace it with the word "`MS-DOS`".
   e. Spell-check to find repeated words. Delete repeated words.
   f. Use the drag and drop method of moving to put each question and the accompanying paragraphs in descending order, i.e. `Question #3, Question #2, Question #1.`
   g. Save the document as CORRECT to the Advantage Diskette.

SESSION 4

WORDPERFECT 6.1 FOR WINDOWS: PRINTING AND FILE MANAGEMENT COMMANDS

Before computers, the production process for creating, typesetting, and printing documents required weeks of detailed work. Many of these steps are now handled automatically by word processing programs. The formatting, printing, and file management tools available in these programs have redefined the marketplace for commercial printers and publishers.

PREVIEW

When you have completed this session, you will be able to:

Customize and change the view of a document

•

Prevent widows and orphans

•

Insert page numbers

•

Create headers and footers

•

Print a document

•

Copy and delete files

SESSION OUTLINE

WHY IS THIS SESSION IMPORTANT?

After the final editing and proofing of a document, there remain only a few optional steps for finalizing its appearance, and WordPerfect for Windows has tools to help. First, make sure that there are no straggling lines separated from their paragraphs at the bottom or top of pages. Second, place a page number or a section title in the header or footer of pages to guide the reader. Remember that a document is created to be read. Therefore, keep your audience in mind when finalizing the format of your documents.

Besides discussing how to place the final touches on a document, this session introduces several printing and file management commands. To work efficiently with a word processing software program, you must know how to find, copy, and print a document without having to open each file on your hard disk. This session provides you with the knowledge and experience to perform these functions confidently.

Before proceeding, make sure the following are true:

1. You have loaded WordPerfect 6.1 for Windows.
2. You have an empty document displayed.
3. Your Advantage Diskette is inserted into drive A: or drive B:. You will save your work onto the diskette and retrieve files that have been created for you. (*Note*: The Advantage Diskette can be duplicated by copying all the files from your instructor's Master Advantage Diskette.)

WORKING IN DRAFT MODE

As you have experienced in the previous sessions, WordPerfect for Windows has many advantages over character-based word processing programs. One advantage is that WordPerfect enables you to view your document exactly as it will appear when printed. For example, you are able to see such features as the document's margins and its headers and footers (we describe these shortly). To work faster, you can turn off the display of some of these print characteristics by choosing View, Draft from the Menu bar.

To practice displaying a document in draft mode, perform the following steps.

1. Make sure that the Advantage Diskette is inserted into drive A: or drive B:.

2. Open the NEWSLETR document from the Advantage Diskette.

3. Change to the draft mode:
   CHOOSE: View, Draft
   The document looks very similar, but the top margin isn't displaying (Figure 4.1).

4. Remove the draft display mode:
   CHOOSE: View, Page

5. Close the document and don't save any changes.

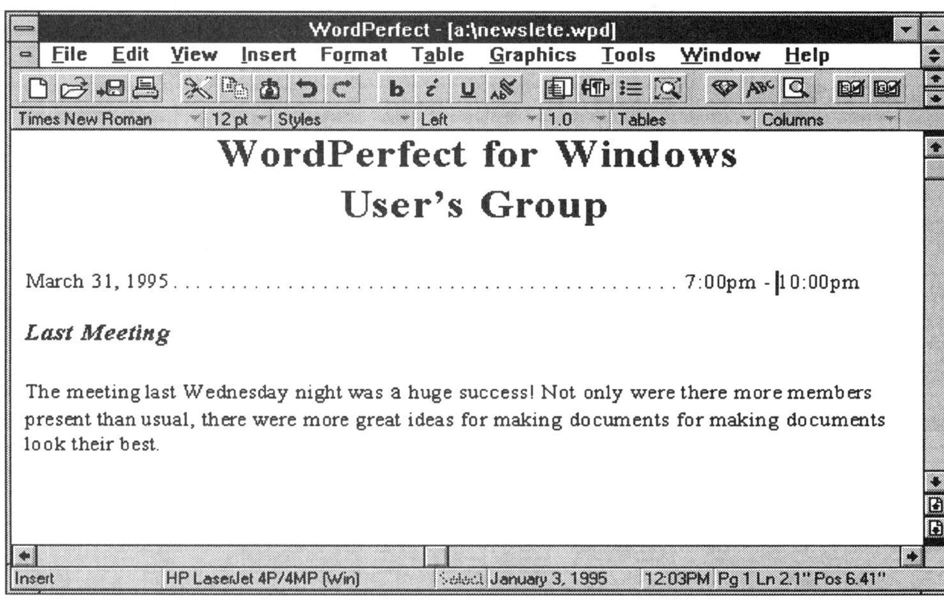

Figure 4.1

Draft mode view of the NEWSLETR document

Quick Reference
Displaying a Document in Draft Mode

To display a document in draft mode:
CHOOSE: View, Draft
After displaying a document in draft mode, to display it in page mode:
CHOOSE: View, Page

DOCUMENT FORMATTING COMMANDS

Having covered character and paragraph formatting in Session 2, in this section we complete the discussion of formatting. Document formatting involves preparing a document for the printer. This section discusses margins, widows and orphans, page numbering, and headers and footers.

CAUTION: As with other formatting commands that we've described (in Session 2), you must position the cursor where you want the command to begin affecting your document. The document is affected from the current cursor position downward. Therefore, if you want a command to affect an entire document, position the cursor at the top of the document before executing the command.

CHANGING MARGINS

Unless you issue a command to change the margins, WordPerfect will print your documents with 1-inch margins on all sides of your text. Depending on your needs, you may want to change the margins to be either larger or smaller. For example, this guide was printed with a 2½-inch left margin so notes could be written there. Users often change the top or bottom margin to ½-inch when they include page numbers in their documents (you learn how to include page numbers shortly.) Otherwise, the page number prints too far from the edge of the page. To change margins, choose the Margins option from the Format pull-down menu. The new margin size must be typed in using tenths of an inch. For example, if you want a margin to be 2½-inches wide, you would type `2.5` for the new margin size.

You can apply different margin settings to different sections in your document. Remember, before you can change the margins of a block of text, you must select it. Otherwise, the entire document is affected downward from where the margin change code is inserted. The margin setting code can be inserted either before or after text is typed.

In this step you will change the left margin of the entire WPBLOCK document from 1 inch to 2 inches. Therefore, before you issue the MARGINS command, you must position the cursor at the top of the document.

1. Open the WPBLOCK document from the Advantage Diskette.

2. To make sure the cursor is at the top of the document:
   PRESS: Ctrl+Home

3. To change the left margin to 2 inches:
   CHOOSE: Format, Margins

4. WordPerfect is now waiting for you to type in a number corresponding to the new left margin (2 inches).
   TYPE: 2
   To return to the document:
   PRESS: Enter or CLICK: OK

5. The document should now be displaying on the screen. Note that the Position indicator on the right side of the status line indicates that the cursor is in position 2" (Figure 4.2).

Figure 4.2

The left margin of the entire WPBLOCK document has been changed from 1 inch to 2 inches.

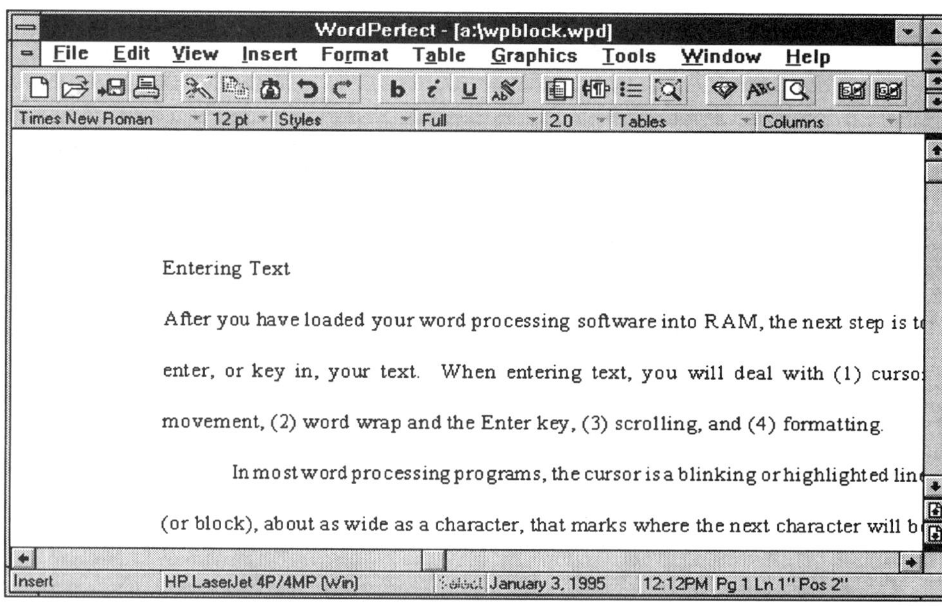

Quick Reference
Changing Margins

1. Position the cursor where the margin change should begin taking effect.
2. CHOOSE: Format, Margins
3. Select Left, Right, Top, and/or Bottom and then type in a number that corresponds to a new column width. Then press Enter to return to the document.

6. To see the margin-change code that WordPerfect inserted in your document, use the REVEAL CODES command (the REVEAL CODES command was described in Session 2):
   CHOOSE: View, Reveal Codes (*or* PRESS: Alt+F3)
   When the cursor is to the right of the margin-change code, it looks like [Lft Mar]. When the cursor is to the left of the code, it looks like [Lft Mar: 2"]. Any text you type at this point will adhere to this margin setting unless you either delete the margin-change code using the Reveal Codes screen or insert another margin-change code below.

If you decide later that you don't want the margins to be changed, you can delete the code. To practice the process, in the following step you will delete the margin-change code.

7. With the codes revealed, the cursor should be to the left of the "E" of "Entering Text." To delete the margin-change code:
   PRESS: ← *until the cursor is to the left of the [Lft Mar] code*
   PRESS: Delete
   The left margin is now 1 inch.

8. To turn the REVEAL CODES command off:
   CHOOSE: View, Reveal Codes (*or* PRESS: Alt+F3)

PREVENTING WIDOWS AND ORPHANS

Although this section heading infers a plan for abolishing family suffering, the section deals with a much less traumatic topic — straggling lines that are separated from their paragraphs by a page break. A **widow** is created when the last line in a paragraph flows to the top of the next page. An **orphan** is created when the first line of a paragraph is the last line of a page. Ideally, a document should not contain any widows or orphans.

When a single sentence is separated from a paragraph, the reader must work harder to keep up with the flow of the text. Fortunately, WordPerfect has a widow and orphan protection feature that automatically prevents these breaks from occurring. Choose Format, Page from the menu and then choose "Keep Text Together" to access the Widow/Orphan option. Remember that the cursor must be positioned at the top of the document if you want the entire document to adhere to the widow/orphan code. Also, before you can change the widow/orphan status of a block of text, you must select it.

Perform the following steps to enable Widow/Orphan protection.

1. If WPBLOCK isn't already displaying on your screen, open the WPBLOCK document from the Advantage Diskette.

2. A widow exists on the top of page 5. One way to see the widow is to display the document in two-page mode and then press **PgDn** until you see page 5.
   CHOOSE: View, Two Page
   PRESS: **PgDn** *three times*
   The screen should look like Figure 4.3.

Figure 4.3

A widow is displaying on page 5.

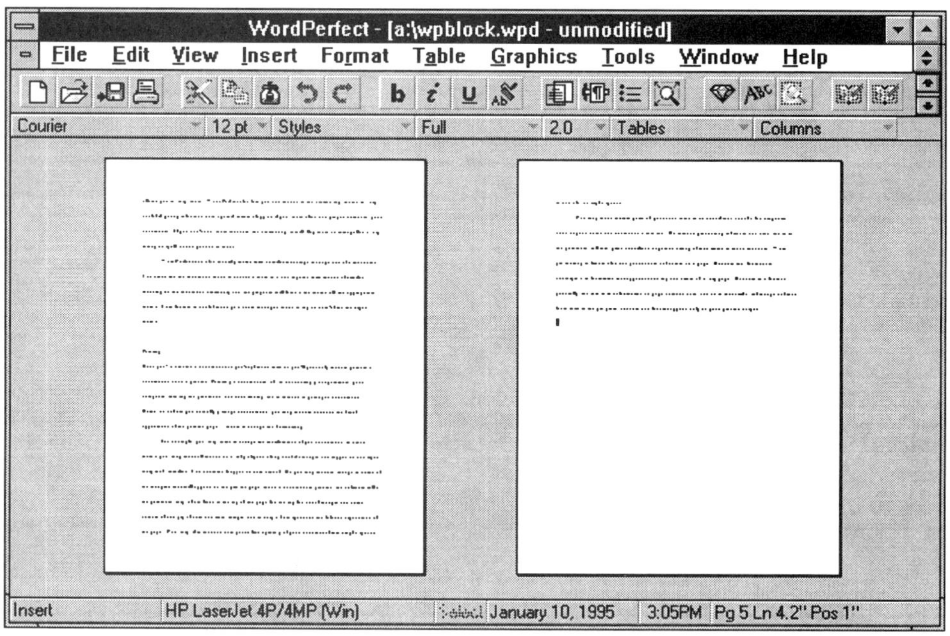

3. To display the document in page mode:
   CHOOSE: View, Page

4. To protect against widows and orphans, first position the cursor at the top of the WPBLOCK document so the entire document is affected:
   PRESS: **Ctrl**+**Home**
   CHOOSE: Format, Page, Keep Text Together

5. The Keep Text Together dialog box is displaying.
   CLICK: Widow/Orphan check box
   PRESS: **Enter** or CLICK: OK

6. To see if the widow no longer exists:
   CHOOSE: View, Two Page
   PRESS: PgDn *three times*
   The widow should have disappeared.

7. To view the document in page mode:
   CHOOSE: View, Page

Quick Reference
Protecting against Widows and Orphans

1. Position the cursor at the top of the document if you want the widow/orphan protection code to affect the entire document.
2. CHOOSE: Format, Page, Keep Text Together
   CLICK: Widow/Orphan check box
   PRESS: Enter or CLICK: OK

INSERTING PAGE NUMBERS

Page numbers assist a reader in finding and referencing sections within a document. In WordPerfect, you can position page numbers at the top or bottom of a document, and align the page number with the left, center, or right margins. Furthermore, you can select the format and starting page for the numbering scheme based on personal preference. For example, you can use standard numbers (1, 2, 3 . . .) or roman numerals (i, ii, iii . . .) for the numbering format and change the format for different sections in a document.

To add page numbers to a document, choose Format, Page, Numbering from the menu. Once the dialog box appears, specify the position and alignment for the page numbers. WordPerfect uses the default format of standard numbers (1, 2, 3 . . .), starting at page 1, unless you specify an alternative.

Perform the following steps to add page numbers to the WPBLOCK document. This document should still be open from the previous exercise.

1. Position the cursor at the top of the document:
   PRESS: Ctrl+Home

2. CHOOSE: Format, Page, Numbering
   Your screen should now appear similar to Figure 4.4.

Figure 4.4

Page Numbering dialog box

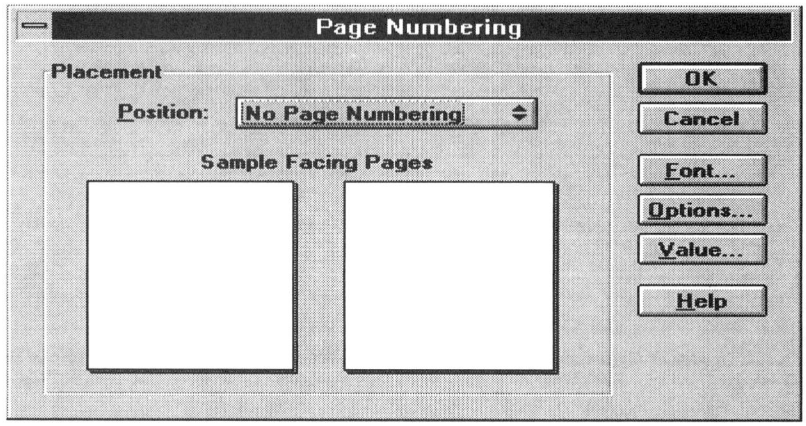

3. To position the page number in the top right-hand corner of the page, point to the triangles to the right of the Position text box and then click and hold down the left mouse button.

4. Drag the cursor down to the Top Right option and then release the mouse button.

5. You can now see the page numbers in the Sample Facing Pages area. To return to the document:
   PRESS: Enter *or* CLICK: OK

6. You should be able to see the page numbers on the screen. If you can't:
   DRAG: *the Thumb on the horizontal scroll bar to the right 1 inch*

Quick Reference
Inserting Page Numbers

1. CHOOSE: Format, Page, Numbering
2. To position the page number in the document, point to the triangles to the right of the Position text box and then click and hold down the left mouse button. Choose a position option and then release the mouse button.
3. To return to the document, press Enter or click on OK.

New Page Number

After you choose Format, Page, Numbering and then choose a numbering option, WordPerfect knows the physical page number of every page in your document and prints the physical page number. In other words, without any special instructions, WordPerfect will print the number 2 on page 2.

In some cases, you don't want the physical page number to print. For example, you might want page numbering to begin with the number 1 on page 2 since page 1 is a title page. Or you may have a large document that has been separated into two or more files. If the first document is 26 pages, you will want the first page of the second document to begin numbering with 27. To change the number that prints, you must choose Format, Page, Numbering, and then click the Value button. Then type in a new page number.

Accompanying Text

WordPerfect enables you to customize the way page numbers appear on the page. To do this you must choose Format, Page, Numbering, click the Options button, and then use the Format and Accompanying Text option. The code that WordPerfect uses to represent the page number is [Pg #]. Unless you make changes in the Format and Accompanying Text dialog box, WordPerfect will print plain pages (1, 2, 3, and so on), as represented by [Pg #]. If you want the page number to print as Page 1, Page 2, Page 3, and so on, type `Page [Pg #]` in the Format and Accompanying Text dialog box. Or if you are printing a 12-page document, type `[Pg #] of 12` into the Format and Accompanying Text dialog box. To change the font of your page numbers, choose Format, Page, Numbering, then click the Font button.

CREATING HEADERS AND FOOTERS

As we described in Session 1, a **header** is information that appears on the top of every page when your document is printed. Textbooks often include the chapter title in the header (called a runninghead) for each page. A **footer** (or runningfoot) is information that appears on the bottom of every page when your document is printed. When adding a header or a footer to a document, position the cursor at the top of the page on which you want the header or footer to first appear.

If [Pg #] is inserted in the header or footer, when the document is printed the current page number will appear. If you know your document is 12 pages long when printed, you may want to include the following footer: [Pg #] of 12. Or you may want to include the following header: Page [Pg #]. Or: –[Pg #]–.

In this section you will add a header that includes the current date to the WPBLOCK document. (*Note*: If you completed the last section, the header will print on the same line as the page number.) Because the header will print on every page, you must first position the cursor at the beginning of the document. Perform the following steps:

1. Open WPBLOCK from the Advantage Diskette (if you haven't already).

2. To position the cursor at the top of the document:
   PRESS: **Ctrl**+**Home**

3. CHOOSE: Format, Header/Footer

4. WordPerfect should now be displaying a dialog box giving you the choice of specifying Header A or Header B. WordPerfect enables you to include different headers on alternate pages. Since you're only including one header, it doesn't matter which option you choose:
   CHOOSE: Header A
   PRESS: **Enter** or CLICK: Create
   The Header/Footer toolbar is displaying below the Power bar.

5. The cursor should have moved into the header area, above the document text. WordPerfect is waiting for you to type header text into the document. To insert the current date:
   CHOOSE: Insert, Date, Date Text
   The current date should be displaying in the header area (Figure 4.5).

Figure 4.5

The current date is displaying in the header.

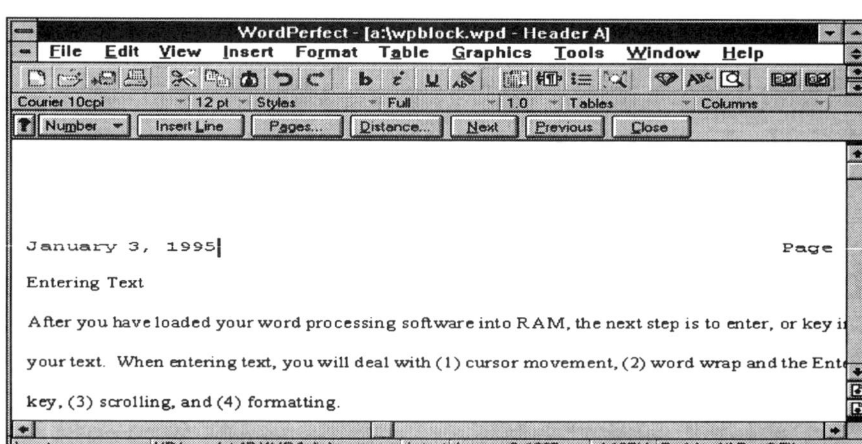

WordPerfect is currently displaying the Header/Footer Feature bar above the header area. The Header/Footer buttons are described below:

- The Number option enables you to add page, section, chapter, or volume numbering inside a header or footer.

- The Line option enables you to add a vertical or horizontal graphics line inside a header or footer. When clicking the Line button the default graphics line is automatically inside your header or footer. To customize the appearance of your line graphic, choose Graphics, Custom Line. The following dialog box displays when you select this button:

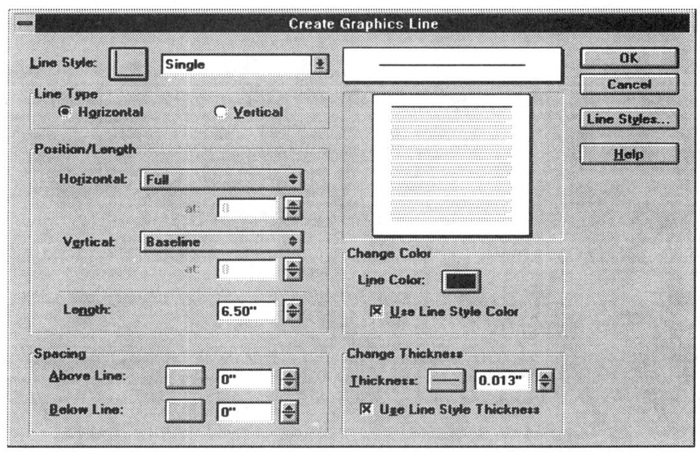

- The Pages option enables you to be specific about what pages the header/footer prints on. The following dialog box displays when you select this button:

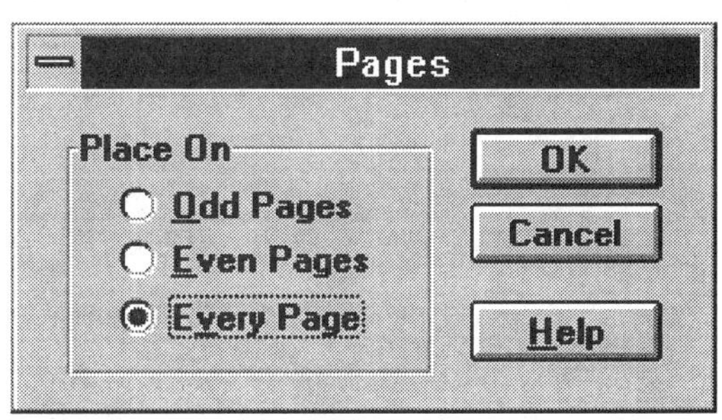

- The Distance option enables you to be specific about how much space is displayed between the header/footer and document text. The following dialog box displays when you select this button:

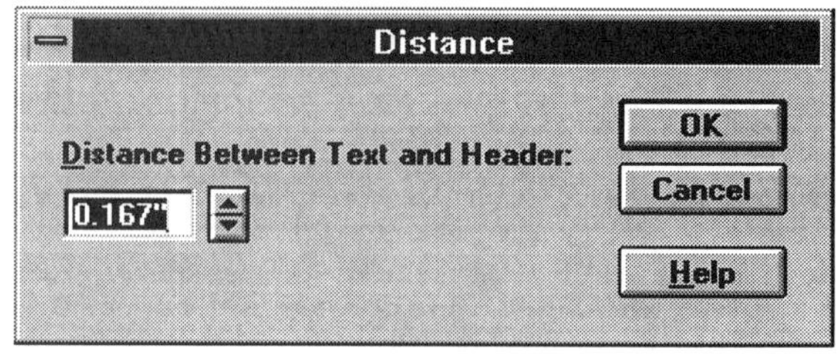

- For documents that contain more than one header/footer, the Next button enables you to move to the next Header A or Header B in a document.

- For documents that contain more than one header/footer, the Previous button enables you to move to the previous Header A or Header B in a document.

6. To display the document:
   SELECT: Close button *located in the Header/Footer toolbar*

7. Close the document and don't save any changes.

Quick Reference
Creating a Header or Footer

1. CHOOSE: Format, Header/Footer
2. Select Header/Footer A or Header/Footer B
3. SELECT: Create
4. Type in the header or footer information and, if necessary, choose one or more options from the Header/Footer Feature bar.
5. When finished defining the Header or Footer, choose the Close button.

CAUTION: When headers are included in a document, you may want to make the top margin smaller. Otherwise too much space appears between the header and the top of the paper. Likewise, when footers are included in a document, you may want to make the bottom margin smaller.

PRINTING A DOCUMENT

In this section, we describe some of the different options available when you print a document. Figure 4.6 shows the Print dialog box that displays after choosing the Print option from the File menu. The Print dialog box is divided into the Print Selection, Copies, and Document Settings sections; these sections display the current print settings and are described in the following sections.

Figure 4.6

Print dialog box

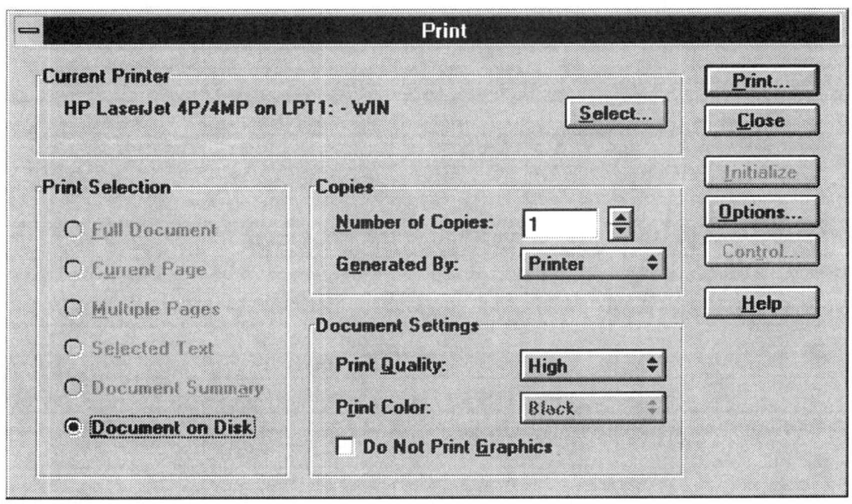

PRINT SELECTION

In this section you specify whether you want to print the full document, the current page (that is, the page the cursor is on), or multiple pages. If you choose multiple pages, WordPerfect will display the multiple pages dialog box after you select the Print button:

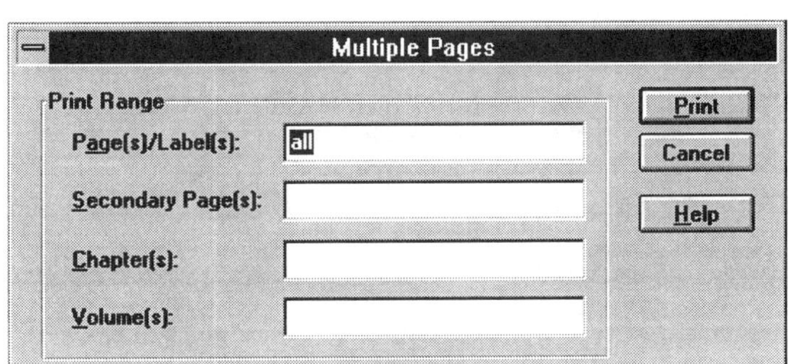

To be selective about the page numbers that print, type the page numbers in any of the following patterns into the Page(s) text box (we use 3 and 5 to represent two page numbers):

3	Prints page 3
3,5	Prints pages 3 and 5
3 5	Prints pages 3 and 5 (same as above)
3-5	Prints pages 3 through 5
3-	Prints the document beginning with page 3
-3	Prints from the beginning of the document to page 3

To print a document that is stored on the disk, select the Document on Disk option, choose the Print button, and then type in a filename. If you had selected, or highlighted, text in the document, you can print the selected text by choosing the Selected Text option; this option will be available to you only if you have selected text in the document.

Printing Multiple Copies

To print more than one copy of a document, choose the Number of Copies option in the Copies list box. Unless you type a number into the Number of Copies text box, WordPerfect will print one copy of your document. To change the way the copies are generated, click on the arrows to the right of the Generated By list box. Your choices are WordPerfect and Printer. If you select the printer to generate the printed copies, WordPerfect sends a page to the printer and the printer prints copies of the remaining pages. It takes less time to print if the printing is generated by the printer. However, the printer can't generate collated copies. It will print all copies of page 1, all copies of page 2, and so on.

Document Settings

The Document Settings list box provides you with options for printing your text and graphics at different resolutions. The quality of a print image is referred to as the **resolution** of the image. High resolution is generally preferable for a final printout. When you click on a triangle next to Print Quality, WordPerfect displays the High, Medium, or Draft options in a pull-down menu.

The Print Color option enables you to print in different colors. You can choose this option only if your printer is capable of printing in color.

FILE MANAGEMENT COMMANDS

Although creating, formatting, and printing documents are definitely major topics in this guide, the importance of file management should not be understated. Without file management commands, you could not back up your work, free up space on a disk for more files, or organize your documents into a logical filing system. WordPerfect for Windows provides several tools for performing common file management tasks. You access these by choosing File, Open and then clicking the File Options button. These file management options are described in the following sections.

COPYING OR MOVING A FILE

Use the Copy option to copy a file to the same disk or a different disk. Select one or more files in the Filename list box and then choose the Copy option. (*Note*: When copying onto the same disk, you must give the copy a new name.) The Move option works just like the Copy option. In this section we lead you through copying a file.

Perform the following steps to make a copy of the file named SAMPLE.WPD onto the Advantage Diskette:

1. CHOOSE: File, Open
   SELECT: SAMPLE.WPD *in the Filename list box*
   SELECT: File Options button
   CHOOSE: Copy

2. WordPerfect is highlighting the filename displayed in the To text box. To copy SAMPLE.WPD onto the Advantage Diskette (that is located in either drive A: or drive B:) as COPYFILE.WPD:
   TYPE: `a:\copyfile.wpd`, or
   TYPE: `b:\copyfile`
   The Copy File dialog box should look like the following:

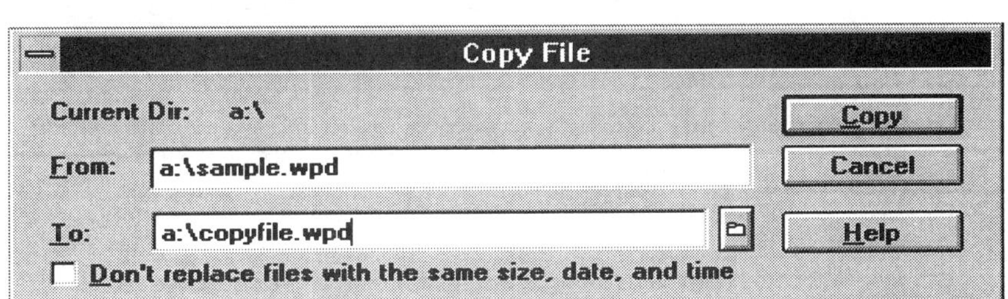

3. To copy the file:
   CLICK: Copy button

4. To display the document screen:
   CLICK: Cancel button
   Note: By clicking the Cancel button, you aren't reversing the last COPY command; you're canceling out of the Open File dialog box.

RENAMING A FILE

Use the Rename option to give a file a new name. Select one or more files in the Filename list box and then choose the Rename option.

Perform the following steps to rename SAMPLE.WPD to NEWNAME.WPD.

1. CHOOSE: File, Open
   SELECT: SAMPLE.WPD *in the Filename list box*
   SELECT: File Options button
   CHOOSE: Rename

2. WordPerfect is highlighting the filename displayed in the To text box. To rename a file and keep it on the same disk, you don't need to specify the drive designation before the filename.
   TYPE: `newname.wpd`
   The Rename File dialog box should look like the following:

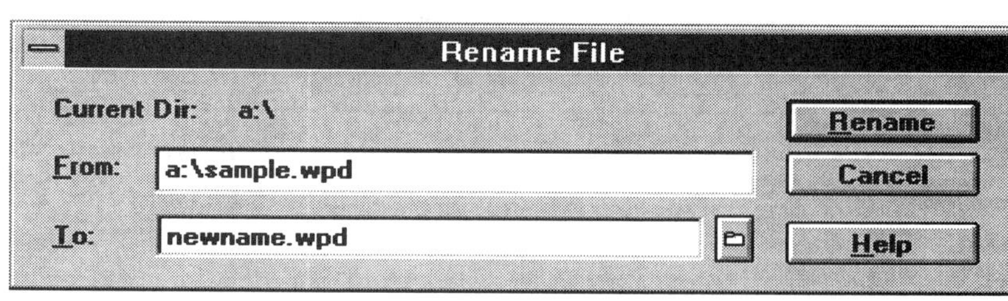

3. To rename the file:
   CLICK: Rename button

4. To display the document screen:
   CLICK: Cancel button
   Note: By clicking the Cancel button, you aren't reversing the last RENAME command; you're canceling out of the Rename File dialog box.

DELETING A FILE

Use the Delete option to delete one or more files from a disk. Select one or more files in the Filename list box and then choose the Delete option.

Perform the following steps to delete the file named OLDFILE.WPD from the Advantage Diskette:

1. CHOOSE: File, Open
   SELECT: OLDFILE.WPD *in the Filename list box*
   SELECT: File Options button
   CHOOSE: Delete
   The Delete File dialog box should look like the following:

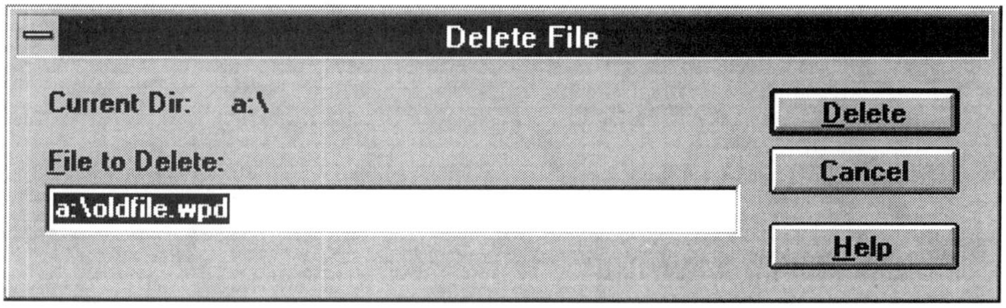

2. To delete the file:
   CLICK: Delete button

3. To display the document screen:
   CLICK: Cancel button
   Note: By clicking the Cancel button, you aren't reversing the last DELETE command; you're canceling out of the Delete File dialog box.

OTHER FILE MANAGEMENT COMMANDS

In this section we describe the Attributes, Print, Print List, Create Directory, and Remove Directory options that are available after choosing File, Open, and then clicking on the File Options button. In addition, the Open as a Copy option is explained.

- Change Attributes. Select one or more files in the Filename list box. Then choose the Change Attributes option. After choosing the Change Attributes option, a dialog box displays that is similar to the following:

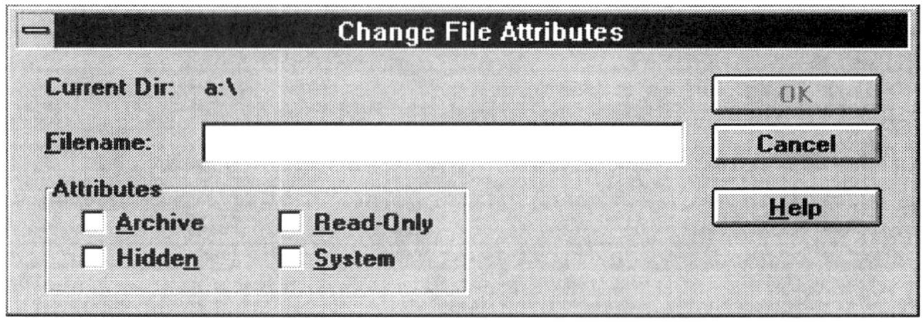

The different file attributes are described below:

Archive	The selected file(s) will be backed up the next time you run a backup program.
Read-Only	The selected file(s) can't be modified or deleted from the disk.
Hidden	The selected file(s) will be hidden from file lists.
System	The selected file(s) will be identified as part of your computer's operating system and won't be displayed in file lists.

- Print. Select one or more files in the Filename list box. Then choose the Print option. The selected file(s) will print.
- Print File List. Using this option you can print a listing of the files that are listed in the Filename list box. You can also select the files to be listed before using the Print List option.
- Create Directory. Using this option you can create a subdirectory on a disk.
- Remove Directory. Using this option you can remove a subdirectory on a disk. Be careful with this command. If you remove a directory that contains files, you won't be able to recover the deleted files.
- Rename Directory. Using this option, you can rename a directory or subdirectory on a disk.
- Open as a Copy. After choosing File, Open, you can open a file as a copy by enabling the check box Open as a Copy. This option is similar to the Save As command in that the file can then be saved as a new name, however the original file is never actually opened.

SUMMARY

This session introduced the document formatting commands for preparing a document to send to the printer. The majority of page layout options are selected from the Format menu. We described changing margins, preventing widows and orphans, inserting page numbers, and creating headers and footers. You also learned that, because the WYSIWYG capabilities of WordPerfect can sometimes slow the data entry process, WordPerfect enables you to view the document in draft mode, which is faster.

The last half of the session examined the printing options and file management commands. Among the printing topics were sections on printing multiple copies of a document and changing the document setting for resolution, or print quality. We also described how to copy, move, rename, and delete files, and how to perform other file management commands.

COMMAND SUMMARY

Table 4.1 provides a list of the commands and procedures covered in this session.

Table 4.1

Command Summary

COMMAND	TASK
View, Draft	Display a document in draft mode
View, Page	Display a document in page mode (margins, headers/footers display)
View, Two Page	Preview two complete pages on the screen at once.
Format, Margins	Change the left, right, top, or bottom margins
Format, Page, Keep Text Together, click Widow/Orphan	Protect against widows and orphans
Format, Page, Numbering	Include a page number in a document

Format, Header/Footer	Include a header or footer in a document
File, Open, File Options & Open as a Copy	Perform file-management procedures such as copying, moving, renaming, and deleting. Open a file as a copy of an original file.

KEY TERMS

footer Descriptive text that appears at the bottom of each page in a document. The footer usually contains page numbers and copyright information; also called a *runningfoot.*

header Descriptive text that appears at the top of each page in a document. The header usually contains titles or section headings; also called a *runninghead.*

orphan A single line that appears at the bottom of a page, separated from the rest of its paragraph on the next page.

resolution Refers to print quality; high resolution is crisper than low resolution.

widow A single line that appears at the top of a page, separated from the rest of its paragraph on the previous page.

EXERCISES

SHORT ANSWER

1. What is the procedure for changing margins in a document?
2. When would you use the Draft mode?
3. When inserting page numbers, when might you want to specify a new page number?
4. What procedure would you use to copy a group of files from a diskette in drive A: to a diskette in drive B:?
5. How do you prevent widows and orphans in a document?
6. How do you insert page numbers in a document?

7. Describe the method for creating headers and footers in a document.
8. What command enables you to view two pages on the screen at once?
9. What procedure would you use to print multiple copies of a document?
10. What procedure would you use to delete a file stored on the diskette in drive A:?

HANDS-ON

(*Note*: In the following exercises, save your documents onto and retrieve files from the Advantage Diskette.)

1. Open SOFTWARE from the Advantage Diskette as a copy. Perform the following steps:
   a. Include a header that displays the current date in the flush-right position.
   b. Protect against widows and orphans.
   c. Left-justify the entire document.
   d. Include your name and the current page number in a footer.
   e. Spell-check the document.
   f. Save the file as MYWARE onto the Advantage Diskette.
   g. Print MYWARE.
   h. Close the document.

2. Choose File, Open to list the files stored on the Advantage Diskette. Then perform the following tasks:
   a. Make a copy of the file named SOFTWARE onto the Advantage Diskette. Name the copy SOFTCOPY.
   b. Rename the SOFTCOPY file to DOC-COPY.
   c. Delete the file named DOC-COPY.

3. This exercise creates a document with headers and footers.
   a. Open a new document by choosing File, New.
   b. Insert 10 blank lines at the top of the page.
   c. TYPE: `BUDGET FORECAST`
      PRESS: **Enter** *twice*
   d. TYPE: `1995`
      PRESS: **Enter** *10 times*
   e. TYPE: `ABC REALTY INC.`
      PRESS: **Enter** *twice*
   f. TYPE: `Sales Team`
      PRESS: **Enter**
   g. PRESS: **Ctrl**+**Enter** *to force a page break*

h. Select all the text on page one of this document and then center it by choosing Format, Justification, Center.
i. At the top of the second page, enter the text appearing in Figure 4.7.

Figure 4.7

BUDGET95 document

```
Introduction

Now that we are in the first quarter of 1995, it is
time we stopped to review our direction for the
remainder of the year. We had a tough year in 1994,
but it seems that the economy is well on its way to
recovery. We are anticipating a good year for all the
staff.

This report is confidential and should not be
circulated outside this office. It is intended to be
a planning document for the Sales Team in 1995. Any
questions or suggestions can be directed to your
immediate supervisor.
```

j. Return to the top of the document.
k. Create the following header and footer. (*Note*: After typing in the text you want left-aligned, choose Format, Justification, Right and then type in the text that you want to be right-aligned.)

Header —	Left-aligned	ABC REALTY, INC.
	Right-aligned	Page *insert page number*
Footer —	Left-aligned	Prepared by: *your name*
	Right-aligned	Printed: *insert date*

l. The header (Header A) should begin printing on page 2 of the document, so you should position the cursor at the top of the first page and then choose Format, Page, Suppress. Click Header A and Footer A.
m. Preview two pages on the screen at once.
n. Print the document.
o. Save the document as BUDGET95.
p. Close the document.

4. This exercise uses some commands (including Format, Line, Tab Set) from previous sessions, as well as document formatting commands.
   a. Open a new document by choosing File, New.
   b. Set the following page dimensions:

Top Margin	1.5"
Bottom Margin	1.5"
Left Margin	2"
Right Margin	2"

   c. Create the following header and footer:

Header —	Left-aligned	`P&L Projection, 1995+`
	Right-aligned	`Page` *insert page number*
Footer —	Left-aligned	`*** Confidential ***`
	Right-aligned	`Printed:` *insert date*

   d. Enter the information in Figure 4.8, using a similar format. *Note*: You'll need to set a left tab in position .5" and a right-aligned tab in position 4.3".
   e. Preview the document by choosing View, Two Page.
   f. Save the document as ABCPROJ onto the Advantage Diskette.
   g. Close the document.

Figure 4.8

ABCPROJ document

ABC REALTY INC.

	1995
Revenue	
Commercial Properties	$125,500,000
Residential Properties	35,000,000
Leased Properties	875,000
Total Revenue	**$161,375,000**
Expenses	
Insurance	$50,000
Salaries	750,000
Commissions	15,500,000
Office Supplies	25,000
Office Equipment	20,000
Utilities	15,000
Leased Automobiles	50,000
Travel	250,000
Advertising & Promotion	25,000,000
Total Expenses	**41,660,000**
Net Income	**$119,715,000**

SESSION 5

WORDPERFECT 6.1 FOR WINDOWS: ADVANCED FEATURES

This session introduces some advanced features of WordPerfect for Windows, including Experts, graphics, tables, merge operations, and macros. Many of these features are useful to the person who wants more from a word processing program than the ability to prepare simple documents.

PREVIEW

When you have completed this session, you will be able to:

Enhance your documents using Expert advice

•

Create a frame for holding a readout or graphic

•

Insert a graphic into a document

•

Create a table for organizing information

•

Merge a list of names into a form letter document

•

Create macros

•

Execute, or play back, macros

Session Outline

- Why Is This Session Important?
- WordPerfect Experts
  - Document Experts
  - Make It Fit Expert
- Inserting Graphics
  - Graphics Boxes
  - The Graphics Box Feature Bar
  - Creating a Image Box
  - Editing the Size of a Graphics Box
  - Deleting a Graphics Box
  - Adding a Graphics Box Style to the Graphics Menu
- Table Fundamentals
  - Creating a Table
  - Resizing a Column
  - Adding/Deleting Cell Lines
  - Shading Cells
  - Table Expert
- Merging Fundamentals
  - Creating a Data File
  - Editing a Data File
  - Creating a Form File
  - Merging the Form File and the Data File
- Macros
  - Creating a Macro
  - Using a Macro
- Summary
  - Command Summary
- Key Terms
- Exercises
  - Short Answer
  - Hands-On

WHY IS THIS SESSION IMPORTANT?

Besides offering helpful techniques to improve your productivity, this session introduces the WordPerfect Experts, graphics and tables. With the capabilities of today's word processing programs, the creation of documents with these features is becoming commonplace. WordPerfect Experts enable you to work smarter and faster. Graphics and tables enhance and clarify points in a document, as well as provide interesting breaks in dense pages of text. WordPerfect for Windows allows you to easily insert and position graphics in a document. This session also shows you how to automate operations in WordPerfect using the merge process and macro commands.

Before proceeding, make sure the following are true:

1. You have loaded WordPerfect for Windows.
2. You have an empty document displayed.
3. Your Advantage Diskette is inserted into drive A: or drive B:. You will save your work onto the diskette and retrieve files that have been created for you. (*Note*: The Advantage Diskette can be duplicated by copying all the files from your instructor's Master Advantage Diskette.)

WORDPERFECT EXPERTS

Word Perfect 6.1 for Windows has added a new feature called Experts to enable you to accomplish more, in a shorter time period. **Document Experts** give you a choice of over 75 pre-formatted professional letters, memos, reports, resumes, fax sheets and more using a simple fill-in-the-blank dialog box. Choose from contemporary, cosmopolitan, traditional or slim-line styles to quickly create matching business documents. Make It Fit Expert shrinks or expands a document to a specified number of pages. The Table Expert makes creating tables a snap by offering many pre-created table styles complete with borders, lines and fills. This section provides examples of Document Experts and Make It Fit Experts. Table Expert will be covered later in this session.

Document Experts

WordPerfect Document Experts allow you to create professional looking business documents using pre-formatted templates. WordPerfect offers not only stylish pattterns for business documents, but also a host of pre-written letters and forms for a variety of business needs. Document Experts are organized in groups such as Business, Calendar and Legal. Within each group are a number of templates to choose from. Pre-written letters such as proposals and job offers can then be easily inserted into your document.

To use the Document Experts, choose File, New from the menu bar, or press Ctrl+T, or click on the document template icon on the Toolbar (). In this section, you will create a letter and a memo, in matching styles, and insert pre-written files into your documents. (*These exercises assume that you have a full, standard version of WordPerfect 6.1 installed on your hard disk.*)

Perform the following steps to create a letterhead in the cosmopolitan style and insert a pre-written job offer and letter closing:

1. CHOOSE: File, New
   The New Document dialog box should look like the following:

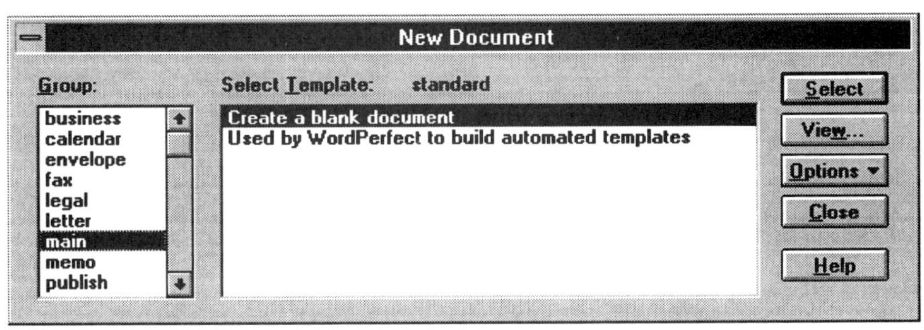

2. SELECT: letter from the Group list box
   SELECT: Letter - Cosmopolitan Letterhead *from the Select Template list box*
   PRESS: Enter *or* CLICK: Select button
   The following dialog box should appear on your screen:

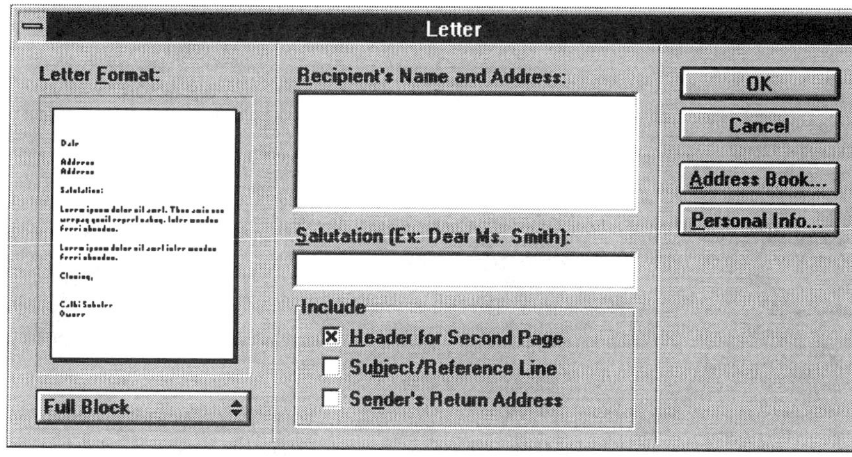

Note: If this is the first time the Template feature has been used on your computer or if an individual's personal information hasn't been entered previously, a dialog box indicating that you must enter your personal information will display. At this point:

PRESS: Enter *or* CLICK: OK

CLICK: Cancel *so that your personal information isn't stored on the computer in your lab*

The dialog box (shown above) should be displaying.

3. Edit the information at the top of the letterhead as follows (this information will be inserted into your document as a header):
   CLICK: Personal Info button
   TYPE*: the following information in the appropriate text boxes as it appears below*:

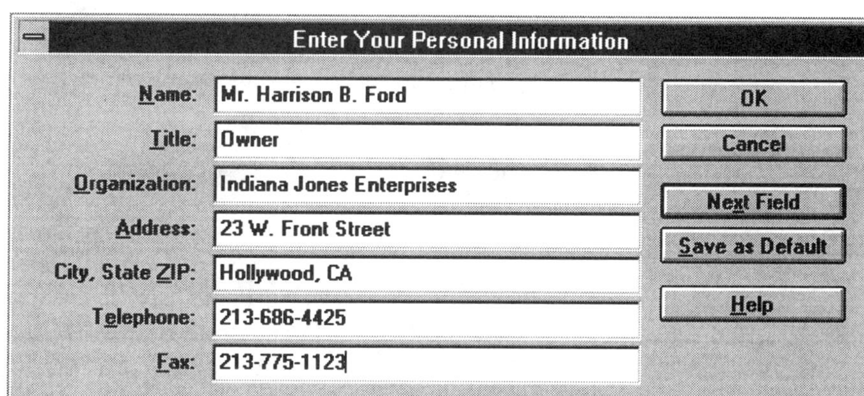

4. If you clicked the "Save as Default" button right now, all letters that you write in the future will be from Mr. Harrison. Currently, Mr. Harrison's information will print in your letters during the current work session.
   CLICK: OK *to continue*

5. TYPE: *your complete name and address* in the "*Recipients Name and Address" text box; press* Enter *after each line*
   TYPE: `Dear` *Your Last Name* in the Salutation text box
   PRESS: Enter or CLICK: OK
   CLICK: OK button *again*
   The introduction as well as the header information now appears in your document.

6. To insert a pre-written letter in your document perform the following steps:
   CHOOSE: Insert, Pre-Written Letter
   SELECT: Job Offer (joboffer.wpd) *from the Filename list box*
   PRESS: Enter *or* CLICK: Insert button
   CLICK: Yes
   Notice that a pre-written job offer has been inserted into your document. WordPerfect has inserted place holders in brackets for you to customize the letter to suit your needs. The inserted portion is automatically centered and formatted to match the rest of your document.

7. EDIT: *the document by selecting the place holders and inserting text of your choice*

8. Insert a closing in your letter as follows:
   PRESS: Ctrl+End
   CHOOSE: Insert, Letter Closing
   CLICK: OK

9. Print the document, close and save the file to the Advantage Diskette as A:LETHEAD.

Perform the following steps to create a memo in the cosmopolitan style using the Document Experts:

1. CLICK: New document template icon on the Toolbar ()
   SELECT: Memo *from the Group list box*
   SELECT: Memo - Cosmopolitan *from the Select Template list box*
   PRESS: Enter *or* CLICK: Select button

2. To insure the header information in the memo is the same as in the letterhead in the previous example:
   CLICK: Personal Info button
   If the header information does not appear as it does on the previous page, enter the information on page 149 in the appropriate text boxes:
   CLICK: OK

3. CLICK: in the "Name of Recipient" box
   TYPE: *your name* in the "Name of Recipient" box
   CLICK: *in the Subject box*
   TYPE: `Job Offer` in the Subject box
   CLICK: OK

4. Insert the file JOBOFFER.WPD into your memo as follows:
   CLICK: Insert File icon on the Toolbar ( )
   DOUBLE-CLICK: Template Directory *in the Directories drop-down box on drive C:, if it is not the current directory*
   (*Note*: In the previous step, make sure you're looking at drive C:.)
   SELECT: joboffer.wpd *from the Filename list box*
   CLICK: Insert
   CLICK: Yes

5. EDIT: *the document by selecting the place holders and inserting text of your choice*

6. Print the document, save and close the file to the Advantage Diskette as A:MEMO.

Make It Fit Expert

Have you ever created a 5 page document, only to have the printed product spill over to 6 pages? Make It Fit automatically adjusts fonts, margins and line spacing so that your document is exactly the number of desired pages. This Expert utility can either shrink or expand a document, depending on your needs. When you choose the Make It Fit icon from the Toolbar ( ), you can specify the options WordPerfect will adjust when fitting your document to a specified number of pages.

Perform the following steps to shrink a document:

1. Be sure the Advantage Diskette is inserted into drive A: or drive B:.
   CHOOSE: File, Open
   SELECT: hardware.wpd from the Filename list box
   PRESS: Enter *or* CLICK: OK
   PRESS: Ctrl+End
   Notice this is a two page document, with the majority of text on page 1 and a small amount of text spilling over to page 2.

2. To shrink this document down to 1 page only:
   CLICK: Make It Fit icon ( )
   The following Make It Fit Expert dialog box should appear:

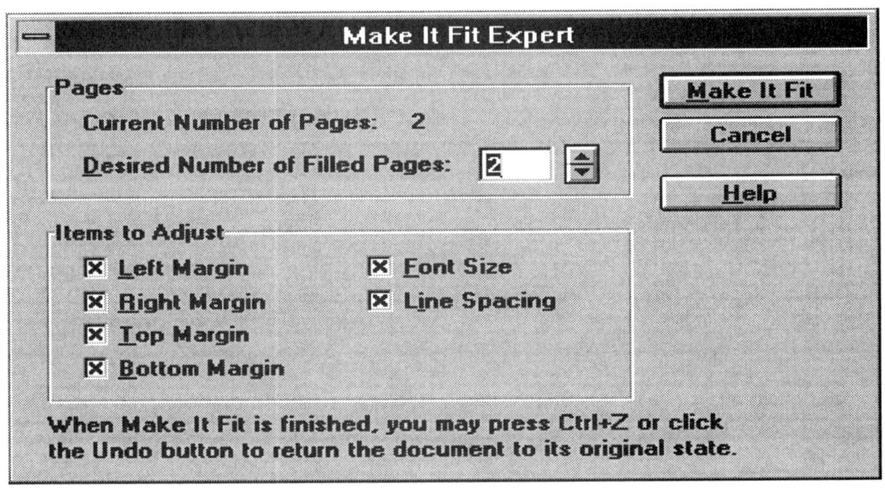

3. TYPE: `1` in the Desired Number of Filled Pages box
   ENABLE: *all the check boxes* under the Items to Adjust box
   PRESS: Enter *or* CLICK: Make It Fit button
   WordPerfect will now adjust the fonts, margins and line spacing to shrink the document to 1 page.

4. PRESS: Ctrl+End
   Notice that the document is no longer 2 pages in length. The font has been slightly compressed and the margins have been adjusted.

5. To return the document to its original state:
   PRESS: Ctrl+`z`, or
   CHOOSE: Edit, Undo

6. Close the document and do not save any changes.

Quick Reference
Make It Fit Expert

1. CLICK: Make It Fit icon ( )
2. TYPE: *number of pages desired*
3. ENABLE: *all the check boxes under the "Items to Adjust" box*
4. Press Enter or CLICK: Make It Fit button

INSERTING GRAPHICS

WordPerfect provides a collection of clip art graphics pictures and borders for insertion into documents. Each of these pictures is stored in a file on a computer's hard disk and has the extension WPG (WordPerfect Graphic). Included in the collection are pictures of a cheetah, hot air balloons, a skier, and a train conductor. Although you would not include these figures in regular business correspondence, they enliven newsletters, brochures, and casual documents. You can practice inserting these fun graphics into a document, using methods similar to those for inserting scanned corporate logos, personal photographs, or maps.

WordPerfect provides two methods for adding graphics to a document:

- The first method involves creating a **graphics box** and then putting text, a clip art image, a chart, a drawing, or an equation into it. WordPerfect provides you with options for specifying the size, position, and one of ten styles of graphics boxes. We describe these in the next section.

- The second method involves retrieving text, a clip art image, a chart, or a drawing directly into your document using the image style of graphics box. This method involves fewer steps than the previous method.

GRAPHICS BOXES

WordPerfect lets you create ten different types of graphics boxes (that you will later fill with something), each with different characteristics: Image, Text Box, Equation, Figure, Table, User, Button, Watermark, Inline and Ole 2.0. (*Note*: The Graphics menu only lists four of the graphics box styles. If you often use a particular box style that doesn't appear on the

Graphics menu, you can add the option to the menu. We describe this procedure later.)

We describe the ten styles of graphics boxes below and provide some examples.

- *Image box*. An image box is used most often with clip art images, charts, logos, or drawings created in a WordPerfect graphics format (.WPG). By default, an image box has invisible borders and no shading. When choosing this box, the Insert Image dialog box appears automatically. The following is an example of a image box that contains a WordPerfect clip art image of a tiger:

- *Text box*. A text box is used most often for quotes, sidebars, or any other text that you want to emphasize. By default, text boxes have a solid line at the top and bottom. The following is an example of a shaded text box:

This text is displaying in a text box that includes 40% shading.

- *Equation box*. An equation box is used most often for mathematical, scientific, or business formulas. An equation box has invisible borders and no shading. An example of an equation box follows:

$$\frac{d}{dx}(au) = a\frac{du}{dx}$$

- *Figure Box*. A figure box is used most often for clip art images, drawings, charts, text, equations, or tables. A figure box is like an image box; however, by default it is a square or rectangle that is framed with a border. To add an image to this box, you must double-click in the graphic box. If you use this box type frequently, you can add the Figure box style to the list of available styles on the Graphics menu.

- *Table box.* A table box is used most often for tables, spreadsheets, statistical data, or text. By default, table boxes possess the same characteristics as text boxes. They're available to you mostly as an organizational tool. For example, in a document about last year's budget, you might emphasize important text in text boxes and budget data in table boxes. By using this organization scheme, you can make a change that affects all the table or text boxes at once (for example, include shading) or more easily locate the graphics item you need to edit or change. If you use this box type frequently, you can add the table box style to the list of available styles on the Graphics menu.

- *User Box.* A user box is used most often for clip art images, drawings, charts, text, equations, or tables. A user box is like a figure box or text box; however, it has invisible borders and no shading. To add an image to this box, you must choose Insert, File from the menu. If you use this box type frequently, you can add the Figure box style to the list of available styles on the Graphics menu.

- *Button box.* Using a button box, you can graphically document a keystroke, push button, or icon. This type of box is similar to the dialog box buttons that you see throughout WordPerfect. If you use this box type frequently, you can add the button box style to the list of available styles on the Graphics menu. The following hypothetical sentence includes a button box:

  Click **Size...** to change the size of a figure box.

- *Watermark box.* A watermark is a graphic (such as a drawing, logo, or clip art image) that is printed lightly behind the text in your document. If you use this box type frequently, you can add the watermark box style to the list of available styles on the Graphics menu.

- *Inline Equation.* An inline equation box is similar to an equation box; however, with an inline equation box you can insert an equation into a line of text. If you use this box type frequently, you can add the inline equation box style to the list of available styles on the Graphics menu.

- *OLE Box*. With an OLE (Object Linking and Embedding) box, you can insert data or an object that was generated in another Windows application directly into your WordPerfect document.

THE GRAPHICS BOX FEATURE BAR

When you create or edit a graphics box, the **Graphics Box Feature bar** automatically displays. If you click with the mouse outside the selected graphics box, the Feature bar is deactivated. (*Note*: If your document contains only one graphics box, the Feature bar remains active even after you click outside the graphics box.)

The options on the Graphics Box Feature bar are used as follows:

Help	Feature Bar help and option.
Caption	Add or edit caption text.
Content	Change the contents of a graphics box (i.e. image, text, equation) and the position of the content within the graphics box.
Position	Change the position of a graphics box on the page.
Size	Change the width and height of a graphics box.
Border/Fill	Change the border or fill pattern of a graphics box.
Wrap	Specify how you want the document text to flow around the graphics box.
Style	Change the box style used for a graphics box.
Tools	Display the Image Tools palette for editing images that are stored in a graphics box.
Next	Move the cursor to the next graphics box in a document.

Prev	Move the cursor to the previous graphics box in a document.
Close	Exit the current graphics box, remove the Graphics Box Feature bar from the screen, and display the document.

CREATING AN IMAGE BOX

In the steps below, we lead you through including a graphic in the file named BIKER that is stored on the Advantage Diskette.

1. Open the BIKER document from the Advantage Diskette.

2. Position the cursor next to the first character (I) of the first paragraph.

3. CHOOSE: Graphics, Image, or
   CLICK: Image button ()
   Notice that the cursor has changed from an I-beam to a hand holding an outlined box. In this mode, you will hold the left mouse button down to drag a box, marking where you will insert the graphic called WINRACE.WPG.

4 CLICK AND DRAG*: the mouse to create an image box no larger than 1/3 of the paragraph*

5. A list of files should now be displaying in the Filename list box. All the files should have an extension of WPG. To bring the WINRACE.WPG image into the BIKER document:

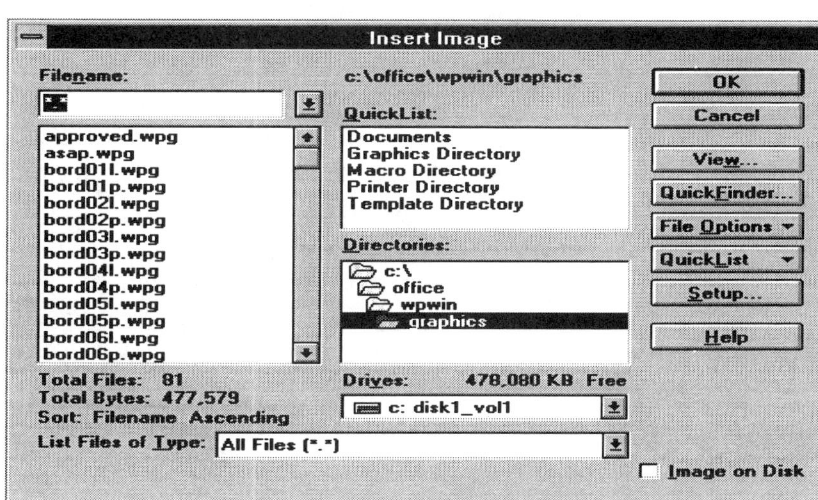

5. A list of files should now be displaying in the Filename list box. All the files should have an extension of WPG. To bring the WINRACE.WPG image into the BIKER document:
   DRAG: *the Filename Thumb to the bottom of the vertical scroll bar until you see WINRACE.WPG*
   SELECT: winrace.wpg
   PRESS: Enter *or* CLICK: OK
   With the cursor near the top of the document, the Document area should look similar to Figure 5.1. (*Note*: The Biker image may be larger on your computer.)

Figure 5.1

Including a graphic in a document

BIKER'S SOURCE

It is my pleasure to announce to the sales staff at Biker's Source that sales have increased steadily for the past six months. As you know, Biker's Source is known for carrying quality sporting items at reasonable prices. But without you, Biker's Source would be "just another sports store." Keep up the good work!

Notice that the graphic defaulted to pre-defined size, regardless of the box size you created using the mouse to click and drag a graphics box. In the next section you are going to resize the graphic box.

5. CLICK: Close *on the Graphics Box Feature bar*
   Keep the BIKER document in the current document area and proceed with the next section.

Quick Reference
Including a Image Box in a Document

1. Position the cursor where you want to position the image.
2. CHOOSE: Graphics, Image, or
   CLICK: Image button ()
3. In the Filename list box, select a file that has the extension of WPG and then press Enter or click OK.

EDITING THE SIZE OF A GRAPHICS BOX

Once a graphics box is selected, you can change many of its characteristics using the Graphics Box Feature bar. To select a graphic, point to the graphics box with the mouse and then click. To deselect a graphic, click anywhere outside the graphic box.

1. Position the mouse pointer in the graphic and then click. Small boxes appear on each side of the image box, which means that the image box is selected.

2. To resize the graphic:
   POINT: *to the bottom-right corner of the graphics box until a diagonal double-ended arrow displays*
   DRAG: *the corner inward until the graphic is the size you want*
   The graphic should be resized.

3. Save BIKER onto the Advantage Diskette using the same name.

Quick Reference
Resizing a Graphics Box

1. Use the mouse to point to the graphics box that you want to edit and then click.
2. Drag a corner of the box inward or outward.
3. When you're done resizing the graphic, click outside the graphic to deselect it.

DELETING A GRAPHICS BOX

To delete a graphic, select the graphic and then press **Delete**. Perform the following steps:

1. The document named BIKER should be displaying on the screen. If not, retrieve it from the Advantage Diskette.

2. Select the graphics box at the top of the document by pointing to it with the mouse and then clicking the mouse button.

3. To delete the graphic:
   PRESS: **Delete**
   The graphic should have disappeared and the paragraph should have aligned within the margins.

4. To restore the graphic to your document:
   CHOOSE: Edit, Undo

ADDING A GRAPHICS BOX STYLE TO THE GRAPHICS MENU

If you use a particular graphics style often, you may want to add it to the menu. By default, only the image, text, and equation box styles are listed in the Graphics menu.

To add a box style to the Graphics menu, perform the following steps:

1. CHOOSE: Graphics, Graphics Styles

2. SELECT: Box
   SELECT: Menu
   The following dialog box displays:

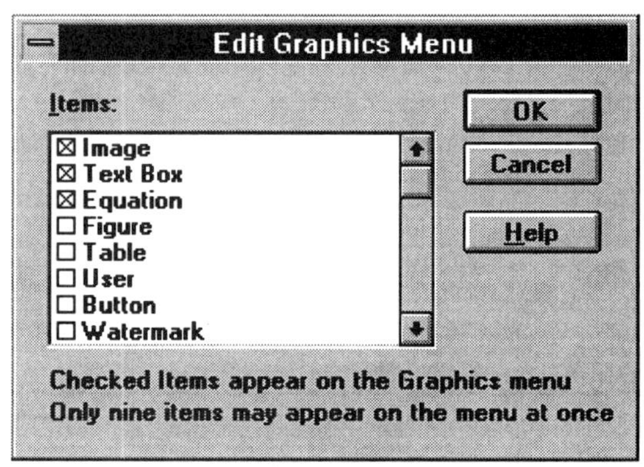

3. At this point you can select the graphics box styles you want to display and deselect the box styles you don't want to display.

4. To display the previous dialog box:
   PRESS: Enter or CLICK: OK

5. To display the document:
   SELECT: Close

6. Close the current document without saving changes.

TABLE FUNDAMENTALS

To organize information into a grid format, WordPerfect provides two options: tabs and tables. You were introduced to defining and using tab stops in Session 2. This section focuses on WordPerfect's table feature. You use a table primarily to line up information into columns and rows. For example, a table works well for creating forms, phone lists, inventory lists, and financial statements. This section introduces you to creating a table, entering information, and formatting a table.

CREATING A TABLE

To create a table, you choose Table, Create from the Menu bar or press **F12**. Then you specify the number of columns and rows desired for the table. Or using the Power bar, you can click the Table button (Tables)and then drag the mouse to select the number of rows and columns you want the table to contain. Adding and deleting columns and rows is quite straightforward, so do not be concerned if you initially misjudge your requirements.

Perform the following steps to create an inventory tracking sheet using the WordPerfect table feature.

1. Open a new document.

2. TYPE: `INVENTORY LIST AS OF MARCH 1995`
   PRESS: **Enter** *three times*

3. CHOOSE: Table, Create
   The Create Table dialog box appears, as displayed below:

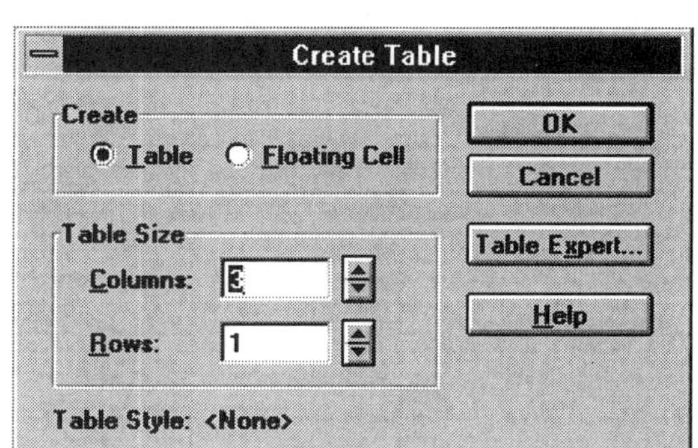

A table is composed of rows and columns. The intersection of a row and column is referred to as a **cell**. In this guide you will be working with table cells and not floating cells. **Floating cells** are a pair of codes that you can insert almost anywhere in your document. You can use them to reference data in a table cell, column, row, or other floating cell.

4. The table you're creating will include three columns by five rows. Note that WordPerfect is already displaying "3" in the Columns box. To enter the number of columns and rows:
   PRESS: Tab *since 3 is already displaying in the Columns box*
   TYPE: 5
   PRESS: Enter *or* CLICK: OK
   A grid pattern appears in the document, outlining the placement of the newly created table.

Quick Reference
Creating a Table

1. Position the cursor where the table should be inserted.
2. CHOOSE: Table, Create
3. Specify the number of columns and rows.
4. Press Enter or click OK.

You enter information into a cell by typing, and advance to the next cell by pressing Tab. To return to the previous cell, press Shift+Tab. Cells within a table can be formatted like any other text in a document.

Perform the following steps.

1. To enter some information into the table, starting with the headings, position the cursor in the first cell in the table:
   TYPE: Inventory Code
   PRESS: Tab
   TYPE: Description
   PRESS: Tab
   TYPE: Quantity on Hand
   PRESS: Tab
   Note that the last Tab takes you to the next row in the table.

2. In the same manner as above, enter the following four items into the table. *Note*: Remember to press Tab to advance to the next cell. If you accidentally press Enter after typing data into a cell, press BackSpace to delete the extra line.

Inventory Code	Description	Quantity on Hand
SVGA-cpd1304	SVGA Monitor	12
CPU-int48666	486/66 MHz CPU	34
HDD-max540	540 MB Hard Disk	12
FDD-teac35	3.5" 1.44 MB Floppy	118

3. With the cursor in the last cell (118), insert a row by choosing Table, Insert. Perform the following steps:
   CHOOSE: Table, Insert
   SELECT: Rows button
   One row will be inserted.
   SELECT: OK button

4. One row was inserted above the last item in the table. To move the cursor to the beginning of the newly inserted row:
   PRESS: Shift+Tab *twice*

   Note: You can delete a column or row by positioning the cursor in the column/row you want to delete and then choosing Table, Delete. Then choose Columns or Rows in the Delete dialog box.

Quick Reference
Inserting and Deleting Rows/Columns

1. Position the cursor in the appropriate row or column.
2. CHOOSE: Table, Insert *or* Delete
3. Click on Columns or Rows.
4. Press Enter or click on OK.

5. Enter one more item:
   TYPE: `VGA-nec4fg`
   PRESS: Tab
   TYPE: `VGA Monitor`
   PRESS: Tab
   TYPE: `15`
   Your document on the screen should look like Figure 5.2.

Figure 5.2

INVENTRY document

INVENTORY LIST AS OF MARCH 1995

Inventory Code	Description	Quantity on Hand
SVGA-cpd1304	SVGA Monitor	12
CPU-int48666	486/66 MHz CPU	34
HDD-max540	540 MB Hard Disk	12
VGA-nec4fg	VGA Monitor	15
FDD-teac35	3.5" 1.44 MB Floppy	118

6. Save the document as INVENTRY onto the Advantage Diskette.

RESIZING A COLUMN

When a table is created, columns are automatically allocated equal widths. You can change these column width settings by positioning the cursor in the column you want to change and then choosing Table, Format.

Perform the following steps to resize the first column in the table:

1. Position the mouse pointer over the cell in the top left-hand corner of the Inventory table that contains the words "Inventory Code." Make sure that the mouse pointer is an I-beam pointer.
   CLICK: *left mouse button once*
   There should not be any cells highlighted in the table—only a flashing cursor in the first cell.

2. To change the width of the first column to 1.75":
   CHOOSE: Table, Format
   The following dialog box should be displaying:

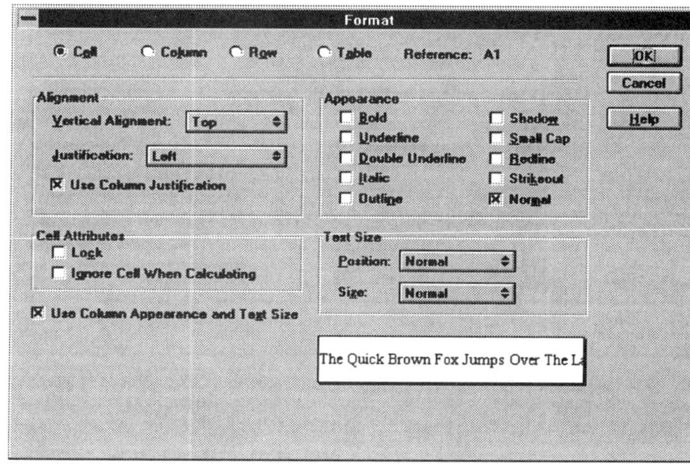

3. To change the width of the current column:
   CLICK: Column

4. Position the mouse pointer over the Width box and then click the left mouse button. Delete the number that's currently displaying (2.17").

5. To set the width of this column to 1.75":
   TYPE: `1.75`
   PRESS: **Enter** *or* SELECT: OK
   The first column has now been narrowed to 1.75".

Quick Reference
Resizing Columns

1. Position the cursor in the column you want to resize.
2. CHOOSE: Table, Format
   CLICK: Column
3. Position the mouse pointer over the Width box and then click the left mouse button. Delete the number that's currently displaying.
4. Type the new width and then press **Enter** or click on OK.

ADDING/DELETING CELL LINES

The gridlines that are displaying around the cells in a table will appear on the printed page unless you choose Table, Lines/Fill to change this setting.

Perform the following steps to take away some of the gridlines surrounding the table data so that the table looks like Figure 5.3.

Figure 5.3

INVENTRY document after lines have been removed

INVENTORY LIST AS OF MARCH 1995

Inventory Code	Description	Quantity on Hand
SVGA-cpd1304	SVGA Monitor	12
CPU-int48666	486/66 MHz CPU	34
HDD-max540	540 MB Hard Disk	12
VGA-nec4fg	VGA Monitor	15
FDD-teac35	3.5" 1.44 MB Floppy	118

1. Position the mouse pointer over the cell with the text "SVGA-cpd1304."

2. Select the data cells by holding down the left mouse button and then dragging the highlight down and across until the five rows of data are highlighted.
3. CHOOSE: Table, Lines/Fill

4. To get rid of the lines on the inside of the table, point to the arrow to the right of the Inside box and hold down the left mouse button. Then choose <None>.

5. PRESS: **Enter** *or* SELECT: OK
   PRESS: *a cursor-movement key so the table isn't highlighted*
   The screen should look like Figure 5.3.

6. Save INVENTRY on the Advantage Diskette and then close the document.

Quick Reference
Adding/Deleting Table Lines

1. Select the cells in the table that you want to affect.
2. CHOOSE: Table, Lines/Fill
3. Make your selection(s) by pointing to the arrow to the right of the appropriate box and then holding down the left mouse button. Then choose an option to affect how the lines are displayed.
4. Press Enter or click on OK.

SHADING CELLS

You can shade table cells by choosing Table, Lines/Fill. Perform the following steps to shade the titles in row one of the table.

1. Select the three cells in row one of the table by holding down the left mouse button and then dragging the highlight across until the three cells are highlighted.

2. CHOOSE: Table, Lines/Fill

3. To shade the selected cells, use the Fill Options area:
   CLICK: the arrow *in the Fill options drop-down box*
   SELECT: 30% Fill

4. PRESS: Enter *or* CLICK: OK
   PRESS: *a cursor-movement key so the table isn't highlighted*

5. Notice that with the shading, the headings are hard to read.
   SELECT: the shaded cells
   CLICK: Bold button (b)
   The screen should look like Figure 5.4.

Figure 5.4

INVENTRY document after shading row 1 of the table

INVENTORY LIST AS OF MARCH 1995

Inventory Code	Desciption	Quantity on Hand
SVGA-cpd1304	SVGA Monitor	12
CPU-int48666	486/66 MHz CPU	34
HDD-max540	540 MB Hard Disk	12
VGA-nec4fg	VGA Monitor	15
FDD-teac35	3.5" 1.44 MB Floppy	118

6. Save INVENTRY on the Advantage Diskette and then close the document.

Quick Reference
Shading Cells

1. Select the cells in the table that you want to affect.
2. CHOOSE: Table, Lines/Fill
3. In the Fill Options area, click <None> in the text box and then select a fill option.
4. Press **Enter** or click on OK.

TABLE EXPERT

As previously introduced in this session, WordPerfect offers Experts as pre-formatted templates to assist you in creating professional looking documents. Table Expert provides many pre-created table styles, complete with borders, lines, and fills. In this section you will use the Table Expert to create the table in the previous examples.

Perform the following steps to create a table using the Table Expert:

1. Open a new document.

2. CHOOSE: Table, Create
   CLICK: Table Expert button
   The following Table Expert dialog box should be displaying:

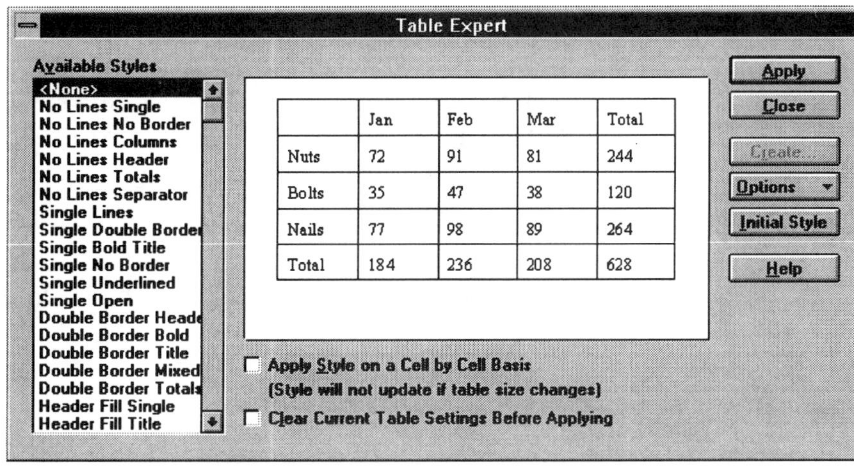

2. A list of available styles is now displayed in the Table Expert dialog box.
   DRAG: *the Available Styles Thumb down the vertical scroll bar until you see Header Fill Double*
   SELECT: Header Fill Double
   PRESS **Enter** or CLICK: Apply button

3. Specify the table size as follows:
   TYPE: `3` for Columns
   TYPE: `6` for Rows
   PRESS: **Enter** or CLICK: OK

4. TYPE: `INVENTORY LIST AS OF MARCH 1995`
   PRESS: **Tab** *once*

5. TYPE: `Inventory Code`
   PRESS: **Tab**
   TYPE: `Description`
   PRESS: **Tab**
   TYPE: `Quantity on Hand`
   PRESS: **Tab**

6. In the same manner as above, enter the following four items into the table. *Note*: Remember to press **Tab** to advance to the next cell.

Inventory Code	Description	Quantity on Hand
SVGA-cpd1304	SVGA Monitor	12
CPU-int48666	486/66 MHz CPU	34
HDD-max540	540 MB Hard Disk	12
FDD-teac35	3.5" 1.44 MB Floppy	118

When complete, your table should look like Figure 5.5.

Figure 5.5

Inventory List created with the Table Expert

INVENTORY LIST AS OF MARCH 1995		
Inventory Code	Description	Quantity on Hand
SVGA-cpd1304	SVGA Monitor	12
CPU-int48666	486/66 MHz CPU	34
HDD-max540	540 MB Hard Disk	12
FDD-teac35	3.5" 1.44 MB Floppy	118

7. Close the current document and do not save changes.

Once you have created a table with the Table Expert, you can apply to your table all the formatting features covered earlier in this session, such as changing column widths and adding cells.

Quick Reference
Table Expert

1. CHOOSE: Table, Create
2. CLICK: Table Expert button
3. SELECT: *One of the pre-formatted table styles*
4. CLICK: Apply button

MERGING FUNDAMENTALS

You probably have received letters in the mail (even from organizations you've never heard of) with your name typed at the top of the letter, in the salutation, and maybe even in the middle of a paragraph. What you received was a form letter. Your name, along with hundreds of others, is part of a data file, and the names in this data file were automatically placed into the letter in predetermined locations through a process called **merging.** Merging involves the use of two files. The body of the letter is referred to as the **form file**. The **data file** contains all the variable data (such as names and addresses) to be included in the document file in the merging process.

When creating a data file, you must define the *records* that you want to store in the file. For example, if you are sending a letter to potential employers, the data for each employer is referred to as a *record.* Each record is made up of *fields.* For example, each employer record might contain name, title, address, city, state, and Zip fields. In the form file, you need to use field codes to indicate what field data (from the data file) should be inserted at that location during the merge process. You create the data file in the next section.

CREATING A DATA FILE

WordPerfect data files are composed of fields and records. You can organize your data files in a text format or in a table format. If you organize the data files in a text format, each field must be followed by the ENDFIELD code, and each record in the file must be separated by an ENDRECORD code. In the table format, each piece of field data is in an individual table cell.

We will now lead you through creating a data file using the text format. You will save it onto the Advantage Diskette as WPDATA. Although most data files contain many records, there are only three records in this file.

1. If you don't have a blank screen:
   CHOOSE: File, New
   PRESS: Enter *or* CLICK: OK button

2. To create a data file named WPDATA, perform the following steps:
   CHOOSE: Tools, Merge

3. Since you are creating a data file:
   CLICK: Data

4. The Create Data File dialog box should be displaying. In this dialog box, you type field names for the different data elements you'll include in the data file. Normally you would determine what names are

appropriate, but for this exercise use the field names given here. Your data file will contain six fields.
TYPE: title
SELECT: Add
TYPE: firstname
SELECT: Add
TYPE: lastname
SELECT: Add
TYPE: address
SELECT: Add
TYPE: city/state/zip
SELECT: Add
TYPE: profession
SELECT: Add
The Create Data File dialog box should look like the following:

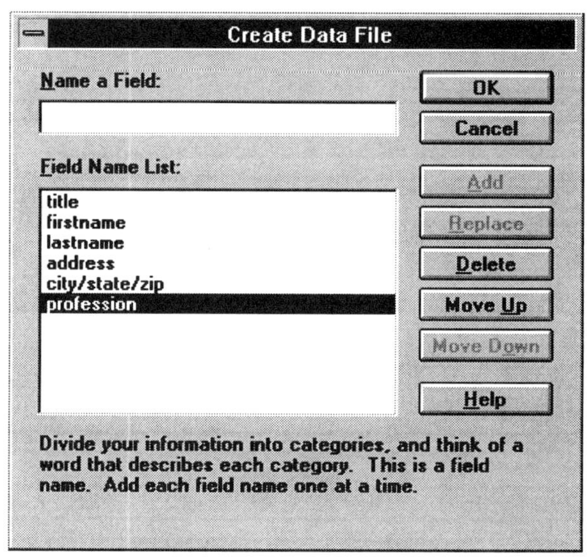

5. Since you're finished defining the field names:
   PRESS: Enter or CLICK: OK
   The Quick Data Entry dialog box should be displaying (see below). Note that the field names you defined in the previous step are displaying on the left side of the dialog box.

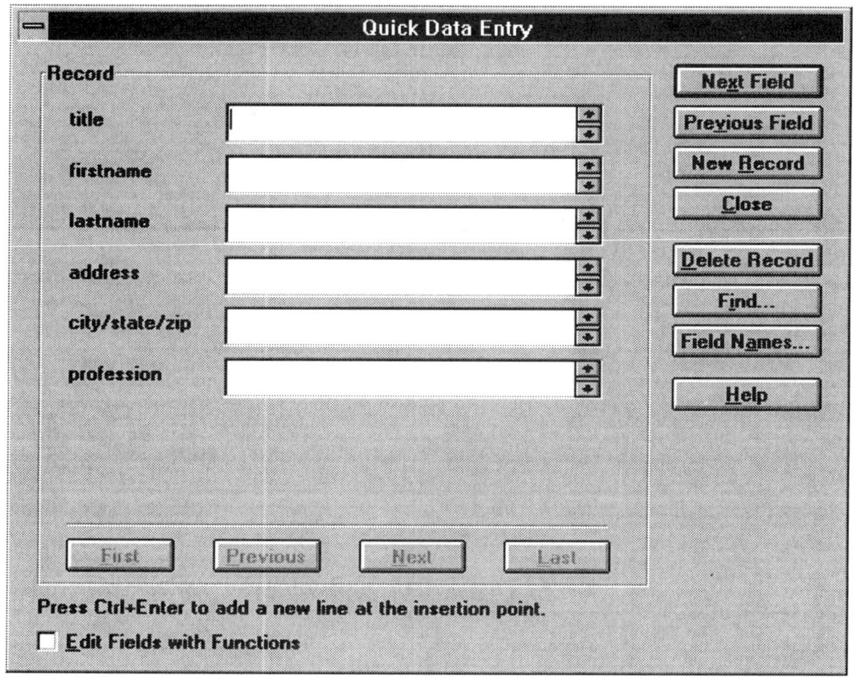

6. To enter the first record:
   TYPE: `Ms.`
   PRESS: **Enter**
   TYPE: `Patricia`
   PRESS: **Enter**
   TYPE: `Stephens`
   PRESS: **Enter**
   TYPE: `1992 Winding Way`
   PRESS: **Enter**
   TYPE: `Chicago, Illinois 60637`
   PRESS: **Enter**
   TYPE: `law`
   PRESS: **Enter**

   A blank form should be displaying so that you can type in the data for record two. *Note*: To view a record you created previously so that you can make changes, select the Previous button, located on the bottom of the Quick Data Entry dialog box. Then choose Next before proceeding.

7. To enter the second record:
   TYPE: `Mr.`
   PRESS: **Enter**
   TYPE: `Jack`
   PRESS: **Enter**

TYPE: `Yee`
PRESS: Enter
TYPE: `392 Riverbend Drive`
PRESS: Enter
TYPE: `Chicago, Illinois 60637`
PRESS: Enter
TYPE: `medical`
PRESS: Enter

8. To enter the third record:
   TYPE: `Ms.`
   PRESS: Enter
   TYPE: `Dalila`
   PRESS: Enter
   TYPE: `Fernandez`
   PRESS: Enter
   TYPE: `3621 Rothwell Court`
   PRESS: Enter
   TYPE: `Chicago, Illinois 60637`
   PRESS: Enter
   TYPE: `engineering`
   PRESS: Enter

9. Because you're done entering data:
   SELECT: Close

10. WordPerfect now wants to know if you want to save your changes to disk.
    CLICK: Yes
    TYPE: `WPDATA`
    PRESS: Enter or CLICK: OK

    With your cursor at the top of the document, your screen should look similar to Figure 5.6.

Figure 5.6

WPDATA data file (partial view). This data file contains three records that will be merged into the form file called SEMINAR.

```
FIELDNAMES(title;firstname;lastname;address;city/state/zip;profession)ENDRECORD
Ms.ENDFIELD
PatriciaENDFIELD
StephensENDFIELD
1992 Winding WayENDFIELD
Chicago, Illinois 60637ENDFIELD
lawENDFIELD
ENDRECORD
Mr. ENDFIELD
JackENDFIELD
YeeENDFIELD
392 Riverbend DriveENDFIELD
Chicago, Illinois 60637ENDFIELD
medicalENDFIELD
ENDRECORD
Ms. ENDFIELD
DalilaENDFIELD
```

11. Close the document window.
    CHOOSE: File, Close

Quick Reference
Creating a Data File

1. CHOOSE: Tools, Merge
   CHOOSE: Data
2. Type each field name and press Enter (or choose Add) after each one. When finished, press Enter or Click OK.
3. Type the field data and press Enter after each field. Continue until all records are entered. When finished, select Close.
4. When WordPerfect prompts you to save your work, choose Yes and then save the data file.

EDITING A DATA FILE

To edit a data file, retrieve the file into a Document window. Select the Quick Entry button located below the Power bar. The first record in the data file will display on the screen. To display additional records, click Next. To display previous records, click Previous. When you're finished making changes to the data file, click Close. Choose Yes to save changes.

CREATING A FORM FILE

In this section you will retrieve the letter pictured in Figure 5.7 from the Advantage Diskette. Then you will modify it so that it can be used as the form file in a merge.

Figure 5.7

SEMINAR

March 27, 1995

Ms. Donna Abrahamson
355 Walnut Street
San Francisco, CA 94109

Dear Ms. Abrahamson:

I hear you're in the medical profession! You could benefit very much by attending my free seminar on health and fitness. It will be offered at Sporting Life, on 123 Main Street in Boston. Ms. Abrahamson, if you are interested please call Sporting Life to set up a reservation.

Hope to hear from you soon!

(your name)

1. Open SEMINAR from the Advantage Diskette.
2. Edit the letter to include your name at the bottom (as indicated in the letter).

Perform the following steps to edit the document so that it looks like Figure 5.8.

Figure 5.8

SEMINAR.LET with inserted merge codes.

March 27, 1995

FIELD(title) FIELD(firstname) FIELD(lastname)
FIELD(address)
FIELD(city/state/zip)

Dear FIELD(title) FIELD(lastname):

I hear you're in theFIELD(profession) profession! You could benefit very much by attending my free seminar on health and fitness. It will be offered at Sporting Life, on 123 Main Street in Boston. FIELD(title) FIELD(lastname), if you are interested please call Sporting Life to set up a reservation.

Hope to hear from you soon!

To substitute the appropriate merge code for "Ms." (title field) at the top of the letter:

1. Position the cursor before the "M" of "Ms."

2. To insert the merge code for field one:
   CHOOSE: Tools, Merge

3. Since you're creating a form file:
   CLICK: Form

4. WordPerfect wants to know if you want to use the text that is in the current window. Since you do:
   SELECT: Use File in Active Window
   PRESS: Enter or CLICK: OK

5. WordPerfect now wants to know the name of the data file you'll be using with this form file. Depending on where the Advantage Diskette is located:
   TYPE: `a:WPDATA` or TYPE: `b:WPDATA`
   PRESS: Enter or CLICK: OK

6. Note that WordPerfect is displaying additional button options below the Power bar. To insert the appropriate merge code:
   CLICK: Insert Field button
   The Insert Field Name or Number dialog box is displaying. This box will stay open until all the fields are inserted.
   SELECT: title
   CLICK: Insert button
   To delete "Ms.":
   PRESS: Del *three times*

To substitute the appropriate merge code for "Donna" (firstname field):

1. Position the cursor before the "D" of "Donna."

2. SELECT: firstname *from the Field Names list box*
   CLICK: Insert button
   To delete "Donna":
   PRESS: Del *five times*

To substitute the appropriate merge code for "Abrahamson" (lastname field):

1. Position the cursor before the "A" of "Abrahamson"

2. SELECT: firstname *from the Field Names list box*
   CLICK: Insert button
   To delete "Abrahamson":
   PRESS: Del *ten times*

To substitute the appropriate merge code for "355 Walnut Street" (address field):

1. Position the cursor before the "3" of "355 Walnut Street"

2. SELECT: address *from the Field Names list box*
   CLICK: Insert button
   To delete "355 Walnut Street":
   PRESS: Del *until the address is deleted*

To substitute the appropriate merge code for "San Francisco, CA 94109" (city/state/zip field):

1. Position the cursor before the "S" of "San Francisco, CA 94109."

2. SELECT: city/state/zip *from the Field Names list box*
   CLICK: Insert button
   To delete "San Francisco, CA 94109":
   PRESS: Del *until the city, state, and Zip information is deleted*

To substitute the appropriate merge code for "Ms." in the salutation:

1. Position the cursor before the "M" of "Ms.".

2. SELECT: title *from the Field Names list box*
   CLICK: Insert button
   To delete "Ms.":
   PRESS: Del *three times*

To substitute the appropriate merge code for "Abrahamson" in the salutation:

1. Position the cursor before the "A" of "Abrahamson."

2. SELECT: lastname *from the Field Names list box*
   CLICK: Insert button
   To delete "Abrahamson":
   PRESS: **Del** *ten times*

To substitute the appropriate merge code for "medical" (profession field) in the first sentence:

1. Position the cursor before the "m" of "medical"

2. SELECT: profession *from the Field Names list box*
   CLICK: Insert button
   To delete "medical":
   PRESS: **Del** *seven times*

To substitute the appropriate merge code for "Ms." (title field) in the last sentence:

1. Position the cursor before the "M" of "Ms." *Note*: The text may have scrolled off the screen to the right. If necessary, press **End** to move the cursor so you can see the right side of the document.

2. SELECT: title *from the Field Names list box*
   CLICK: Insert button
   To delete "Ms.":
   PRESS: **Del** *three times*

To substitute the appropriate merge code for "Abrahamson" (lastname field):

1. Position the cursor before the "A" of "Abrahamson."

2. SELECT: lastname *from the Field Names list box*
   CLICK: Insert button
   To delete "Abrahamson":
   PRESS: **Delete** *ten times*
   CLICK: Close button

   Don't worry if the right margins appear to be out of alignment. When printed, each letter will be aligned.

3. Save this document onto the Advantage Diskette as FORMLET. (Remember to use the SAVE AS command.)

4. Close the Document window.

Quick Reference
Creating a Form File

To insert merge codes in your document:

1. CHOOSE: Tools, Merge
2. CLICK: Use File in Active Window, or
   CLICK: New Document Window
   PRESS Enter or, CLICK: OK
3. TYPE: the name of the data file
   CLICK: OK
4. Position the cursor where a merge code should be inserted.
   CLICK: Insert Field button
   SELECT: a field name
   CLICK: Insert
5. Repeat steps 4–5 until all merge codes have been inserted.
6. CLICK: Close

MERGING THE FORM FILE AND THE DATA FILE

The process for merging a form file and a data file is as follows:

- Make sure all Document windows have been closed.
- Choose Tools, Merge, Merge.
- Type the disk drive designation and name of the form file (FORMLET) and then press Enter.
- Type the disk drive designation and name of the data file (WPDATA) and then press Enter.

Perform the following steps to merge FORMLET with WPDATA:

1. The Document window should be empty.
   CHOOSE: Tools, Merge, Merge
   The Perform Merge dialog box is displaying.

2. WordPerfect is now prompting you to enter the disk drive designation and name of the form file.
   TYPE: A:FORMLET *or* B:FORMLET
   PRESS: Tab

3. WordPerfect is now prompting you to enter the name of the data file.
   TYPE: A:WPDATA *or* B:WPDATA
   PRESS: Enter or CLICK: OK

When the merge is complete, your cursor is positioned at the end of all the merged documents. To see the documents, press PgUp. Note that the names and addresses were replaced by the names and addresses in your data file, and the profession data was merged into the first line of the letter. In addition, the title and lastname fields were merged into the last line of the letter.

Now that the merging process is complete, you have a few options: (1) if you want to view the letters on paper, print them out; (2) save the letters onto a data diskette and print them later; or (3) clear RAM and merge the two files later.

4. At this point, close all open windows and do not save changes.

Quick Reference
Performing a Merge

1. Make sure that a blank Document window is displaying on the screen.
2. CHOOSE: Tools, Merge, Merge
3. Type in the disk drive designation and name of the form file.
4. PRESS: Tab
5. Type in the disk drive designation and name of the data file.
6. PRESS: Enter

MACROS

Macros are used to automate frequently used procedures. For example, if you always type the same text (such as the name and address of the company you're working for) into multiple documents, you can use a macro to automate the procedure of typing in the text. Or, if you often find it necessary to make the same formatting changes in your documents, such as a line spacing or tab line change, you can automate these procedures with a macro. In the sections below you learn how to create and use macros.

CREATING A MACRO

The procedure of creating a macro involves the following:

- Choose Tools, Macro, Record.
- Type a name for the macro in the Filename box.
- Click the Record button.
- Perform the procedure you want to automate.
- To stop the recording process, choose Tools, Macro, Record.

Pretend that you frequently send business letters to Harold Trimalski. Perform the following steps to create a macro named WPBEGIN that automates the procedure of typing the beginning of a letter which includes the current date, Mr. Trimalski's name and address, and the salutation.

1. If necessary, open a new document.

2. To initiate the MACRO command:
   CHOOSE: Tools, Macro, Record
   The Record Macro dialog box pictured below should be displaying:

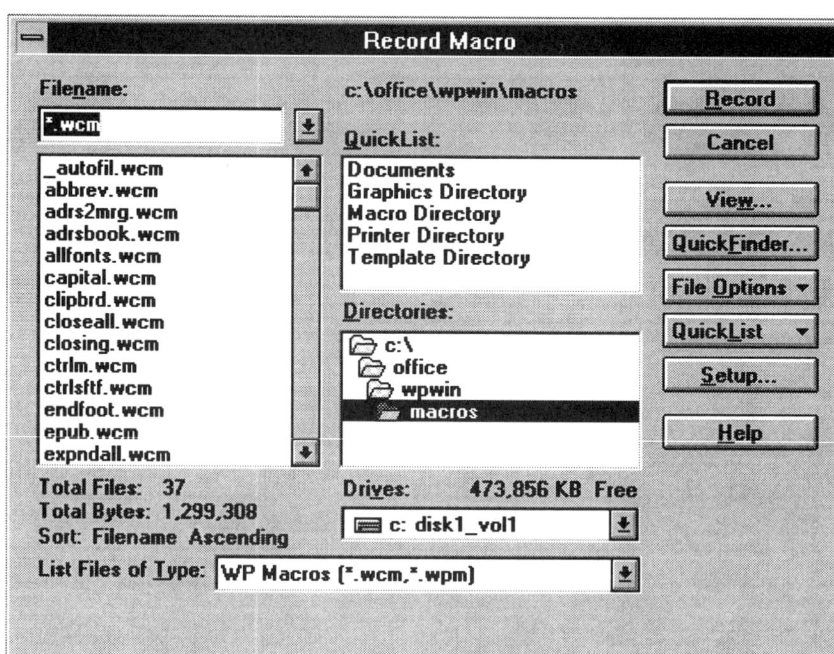

3. WordPerfect is waiting for you to assign a name to the macro. *(Note: all previously recorded macros are listed as well in the Filename list box.)*
   TYPE: `A:WPBEGIN` *or* `B:WPBEGIN`
   PRESS: Enter or CLICK: Record

4. The text "Macro Record" should be displaying in the lower left-hand corner. Every keystroke you type now will be stored in the macro until you choose Tools, Macro, Record. If you make mistakes while typing, correct them as you normally would.

5. To include the current date, a name and address, and a salutation at the top of the document, perform the following steps:
   CHOOSE: Insert, Date, Date Text
   PRESS: Enter *four times*
   TYPE: `Mr. Harold Trimalski`
   PRESS: Enter
   TYPE: `XYZ Corporation`
   PRESS: Enter
   TYPE: `199 E. Spalding Avenue, Suite 1440`
   PRESS: Enter
   TYPE: `Chicago, Illinois 60637`
   PRESS: Enter *twice*
   TYPE: `Dear Mr. Trimalski:`
   PRESS: Enter *twice*

6. To stop WordPerfect from recording the macro:
   CHOOSE: Tools, Macro, Record
   The macro has now been saved onto the Advantage Diskette. WordPerfect automatically supplied the extension of WCM to your macro name (WPBEGIN.WCM).

7. Close the current document without saving.

Quick Reference
Creating a Macro

1. CHOOSE: Tools, Macro, Record
2. TYPE: *`a macro name`*
3. PRESS: Enter *or* CLICK: Record button
4. Perform the procedure you want to automate.
5. When finished performing the procedure:
   CHOOSE: Tools, Macro, Record

USING A MACRO

In this section you will use the WPBEGIN.WPM macro. Make sure the screen is cleared before performing the following procedure.

1. CHOOSE: Tools, Macro, Play

2. To select the WCM file you just created:
   DRAG: *the Filename Thumb down the vertical scroll bar until you see WPBEGIN.WCM (you may need to change the current disk drive to the drive containing the Advantage Diskette)*
   SELECT: wpbegin.wcm
   CLICK: Play

The screen should look like Figure 5.9. If you can't see the top of the letterhead, press PgUp.

3. Close the document window without saving.

Figure 5.9

Using the WPBEGIN macro. This is what will appear on the screen after you execute the WPBEGIN macro.

Current Date

Mr. Harold Trimalski
XYZ Corporation
199 E. Spalding Avenue, Suite 1440
Chicago, Illinois 60637

Dear Mr. Trimalski:

Quick Reference
Using a Macro

1. CHOOSE: Tools, Macro, Play
2. If necessary, click the Open icon to the right of the Name box. Select the macro you want to execute.
3. SELECT: Play button

SUMMARY

This session introduced you to some advanced features of WordPerfect, including Document Experts, inserting graphics in a document and creating tables. Graphics and tables, once the domain of commercial typesetters, are now easily added to documents, as demonstrated in this session.

With WordPerfect's automated mail merge feature, you can easily produce form documents. Form documents are standard documents in which only a small amount of information, such as the addressee, changes. With the variable information entered into a data file, only a single form document needs to be created. The process of merging takes the information from the data file and inserts it into the correct locations in the form document.

Another productivity tool, called macros, was also introduced in this session. Macros allow you to automate repetitive tasks that require several keystrokes.

COMMAND SUMMARY

Table 5.1 provides a list of the commands and procedures covered in this session.

Table 5.1	COMMAND TASK	STEPS
Command Summary	Document Expert	1. CHOOSE: File, New from the menu bar, or PRESS: CTRL+T, or CLICK: new document template icon on the Toolbar 2. SELECT: *type of document* from the Group box 3. SELECT: *template* from the Select Template box 4. Press **Enter** or CLICK: Select button
	Make It Fit Expert	1. CLICK: Make It Fit icon on the Toolbar 2. TYPE: *number of pages desired* 3. CHECK: Items to Adjust 4. Press **Enter** or CLICK: Make It Fit button

Including a figure box in a document

1. CLICK: Image button on the Toolbar  or CHOOSE: Graphics, Image.
2. In the Filename list box, select a file that has the extension of WPG and then press Enter or click OK.

Resizing a graphics box

1. Use the mouse to point to the graphics box that you want to edit and then click.
2. Point to a corner of the graphics box and drag the corner inward or outward.
3. When you're done editing the graphic, click outside the graphic to deselect it.

Creating a table

1. Position the cursor where the table should be inserted.
2. CHOOSE: Table, Create
3. Specify the number of columns and rows.
4. Press Enter or click OK.

Creating a table using the Table Expert

1. CHOOSE: Table, Create
2. CLICK: Table Expert button
3. SELECT: a predefined table from the list of Available Styles
4. Press Enter or click Apply button.

Inserting/deleting rows and columns

1. Position the cursor in the appropriate row or column.
2. CHOOSE: Table, Insert *or* Delete
3. Click on Columns or Rows.
4. Press Enter or click on OK.

Resizing table columns

1. Position the cursor in the column you want to resize.
2. CHOOSE: Table, Format
   CLICK: Column
3. Position the mouse pointer over the Width box and then click the left mouse button. Delete the number currently displayed.
4. Type the new width and then press Enter or click on OK.

Adding and deleting table lines	1. Select the cells in the table that you want to affect. 2. CHOOSE: Table, Lines/Fill 3. Make your selection(s) by pointing to the arrow to the right of the appropriate box and then holding down the left mouse button. Then choose an option to affect how the lines are displayed. 4. Press Enter or click on OK.
Shading cells	1. Select the cells in the table that you want to affect. 2. CHOOSE: Table, Lines/Fill 3. In the Fill Options area, click <None> in the text box and then select a fill option. 4. Press Enter or click on OK.
Creating a form file	To insert merge codes in your document: 1. CHOOSE: Tools, Merge 2. CLICK: Use File in Active Window, or CLICK: New Document Window CLICK: OK 3. TYPE: the name of the data file CLICK: OK 4. Position the cursor where a field code should be inserted. CLICK: Insert Field button SELECT: a field name CLICK: Insert CLICK: Close 5. Repeat steps 4–5 until all merge codes have been inserted.
Creating a data file	1. CHOOSE: Tools, Merge CHOOSE: Data 2. Type each field name and press Enter (or choose Add) after each one. When finished, select Close. 3. Type the field data and press Enter after each field. Continue until all records are entered. When finished, select Close. 4. When WordPerfect prompts you to save your work, choose Yes and then save the data file.

Performing a merge	1. Make sure that a blank Document window is displaying on the screen. 2. CHOOSE: Tools, Merge, Merge 3. Type in the disk drive designation and name of the form file. 4. PRESS: Tab 5. Type in the disk drive designation and name of the data file. 6. PRESS: Enter
Creating a macro	1. CHOOSE: Tools, Macro, Record 2. TYPE: *a macro name* 3. PRESS: Enter *or* CLICK: Record button 4. Perform the procedure you want to automate. 5. When finished performing the procedure: CHOOSE: Tools, Macro, Record
Using a macro	1. CHOOSE: Tools, Macro, Play 2. If necessary, click the Open icon to the right of the Name box. Select the macro you want to execute. 3. SELECT: Play button

KEY TERMS

cell The intersection of a column and a row in a table.

data file A document file that uses a table to capture and store variable information for the merge process.

Document Expert Pre-formatted letters, templates and tables that enable you to do more in less time.

floating cells A pair of codes that you can insert almost anywhere in your document. Use these codes to reference data in a table cell, column, row, or other floating cell.

form file In WordPerfect, the form file contains the letter or other document into which data in the data file is inserted during the merging process.

graphics box In WordPerfect, this is an area in your document reserved for text, a clip art image, a chart, a drawing, or an equation.

Graphics Box Feature bar This bar provides many options for position, sizing, and otherwise manipulating graphics boxes.

macro A collection of keystrokes that is recorded for playback at a later date. A macro enables you to perform a series of operations by selecting the macro name from a list.

merging The process of taking information from a data file and inserting it into a form letter document or main file, one record at a time. The results from merging these two files can be sent to a file or the printer.

EXERCISES

SHORT ANSWER

1. What two codes must be included in a data file (text format) that will be used in a merge?
2. What is a graphics box?
3. What is a macro?
4. What are clip art images? How are they used?
5. When would you use a table in a document?
6. How do you change the column widths in a table?
7. What characteristics does a form file used for merging have?
8. Explain the merge process.
9. What control does WordPerfect give you over the grid lines that display in a table?
10. How do you create a macro?

HANDS-ON

(*Note*: In the following exercises, save your documents onto and retrieve files from the Advantage Diskette.)

1. In the following exercise, you create and format a table.
   a. Open a new document.
   b. Create the document appearing in Figure 5.10.

Figure 5.10

ROLAND document

current date

Mr. Roland Garros
Clay Supplies Inc.
1091 Panorama Ridge
Amarillo, TX 76798

Dear Mr. Garros:

Per your request, I am providing a list of the items that you ordered for your office last Wednesday.

Please confirm each item with a check mark in the appropriate column and fax this letter back to me at 817-555-1234.

Yours sincerely,
Grand Slam Computer Sales

your name
Account Representative

c. Insert the following table between the first and second paragraphs.

Client Initial	Qty	Description	Total Price
	5	Laser Printers	$10,250.00
	5	Printer Cables	76.00
	20	3.5" Diskettes	30.00
	5	Windows '95	450.00

d. Insert the following new row between the Laser Printers and the Printer Cables.

	5	Legal Paper Trays	150.00

e. Select the entire table.
f. Apply a thick line style to the outside of the table.
g. Save the document as ROLAND onto the Advantage Diskette.
h. Close the document.

2. The objective of this exercise is to create a macro that automates a routine procedure. Pretend you are in charge of keeping track of sales at a local sporting goods store. At the end of each day you have to type summary comments about sales activity for the current day. Create a macro named GETREADY that can be used to automate the procedure of getting ready to type these comments. The macro should do the following:
   a. Change the spacing of the current document to double.
   b. Protect against widows/orphans.
   c. Use the DATE command to insert the current date in the top left-hand corner of the page.
   d. Create a footer that includes the current page number.
   e. Move the cursor down a few lines and insert a centered title that reads:
      `DAILY SALES REPORT`
   f. Move the cursor down a few lines so you can begin typing.
   Execute the macro.

3. In this exercise, you create a form file and a data file, and then merge the two documents to create a third file.
   a. Open a new document.
   b. Create a data file (the data is pictured below) and save it onto the Advantage Diskette as CUSTDATA.

Given	**Surname**	**Address**	**City**	**State**	**Zip**
Elliot	Lepinski	898 Burrard Avenue	Louisville	KY	40205
Red	Robinson	235 Johnson Street	Washington	DC	20052
Elaine	Maynard	1005 West 9th Street, #705	Baton Rouge	LA	70803
Ranjitt	Singh	1227 E. Cordova Avenue	Tacoma	WA	98416
William	Delaney	36 Primore Road	Wichita	KS	67208
Francisco	Ortez	875 Broadway	Albuquerque	NM	87131
Alice	Chan	29 Redmond Road	San Francisco	CA	92182
Jessica	Thomas	909 West 18th Street, #12	Brooklyn	NY	11225
Jimmy	Kazo	888 East 8th Avenue	Billings	MT	59101

c. Create the form file pictured in Figure 5.11 and save it onto the Advantage Diskette as CUSTFORM. *Where indicated, insert the appropriate codes.*

Figure 5.11

CUSTFORM document

today's date

<<Given>> <<Surname>>
<<Address>>
<<City>>, <<State>> <<Zip>>

Dear **<<Given>>**:

We're Moving!

Please be informed that as of August 31, 1995 we are moving to new premises located at 8030 United Boulevard in Boston.

We are looking forward to this move with great anticipation. Because of your continued support, we are expanding our training facilities to accommodate two training rooms and a board room.

As a result of this move, we will be closed from the third week in August to the end of September. An invitation to the Open House will be forwarded to you, **<<Given>>**, as soon as we are settled.

Let us know if we can do anything for you!

Sincerely,

your name
President

d. Close all documents and then merge the CUSTFORM and CUSTDATA files together.

4. In this exercise you will merge a form file and a data file together to generate form letters.
    a. In this step you will create a data file named DATAFILE that will be used shortly in a merge. Add five records to the data file (you make up the data). Each record contains the following six fields:
        (1) the manager's title
        (2) the manager's first name
        (3) the manager's last name
        (4) the name of the sporting goods store
        (5) the store's address
        (6) the city, state, and Zip of the store
    b. Retrieve the file named WPMERGE from the Advantage Diskette.
    c. Modify this letter so that it contains the appropriate field codes from the DATAFILE data file. (*Note*: Make sure to include the code for the name of the sporting goods store in the first sentence of the document).
    d. Include the current date at the top of the document.
    e. Substitute your name in place of the text "(your name)" at the bottom of the document.
    f. Save WPMERGE onto the Advantage Diskette.
    g. Close all documents.
    h. Save this data onto the Advantage Diskette as DATAFILE.
    i. Close all documents and then merge WPMERGE and DATAFILE together.
    j. Print the merged documents.

INDEX

WORDPERFECT® 6.1